Democracy in Classical Athens

Classical World Series

Aristophanes and his Theatre of the Absurd, Paul Cartledge
Art and the Romans, Anne Haward
Athens and Sparta, S. Todd
Athens under Tyrants, J. Smith
Athletics in the Ancient World, Zahra Newby
Attic Orators, Michael Edwards
Augustan Rome, Andrew Wallace-Hadrill
Cicero and the End of the Roman Republic, Thomas Wiedemann
Cities of Roman Italy, Guy de la Bédoyère
Classical Archaeology in the Field, S. J. Hill, L. Bowkett and K. & D. Wardle
Classical Epic: Homer and Virgil, Richard Jenkyns
Democracy in Classical Athens, Christopher Carey
Early Greek Lawgivers, John Lewis
Environment and the Classical World, Patricia Jeskins
Greece and the Persians, John Sharwood Smith
Greek and Roman Historians, Timothy E. Duff
Greek and Roman Medicine, Helen King
Greek Architecture, R. Tomlinson
Greek Literature in the Roman Empire, Jason König
Greek Sculpture, Georgina Muskett
Greek Tragedy: Themes and Contexts, Laura Swift
Greek Vases, Elizabeth Moignard
Homer: The Iliad, William Allan
Julio-Claudian Emperors, T. Wiedemann
Lucretius and the Didactic Epic, Monica Gale
Morals and Values in Ancient Greece, John Ferguson
Mycenaean World, K. & D. Wardle
Ovid: A Poet on the Margins, Laurel Fulkerson
Plato's Republic and the Greek Enlightenment, Hugh Lawson-Trancred
The Plays of Aeschylus, A.F. Garvie
The Plays of Euripides, James Morwood
The Plays of Sophocles, A.F. Garvie

Political Life in the City of Rome, J. R. Patterson
Religion and the Greeks, Robert Garland
Religion and the Romans, Ken Dowden
Roman Architecture, Martin Thorpe
The Roman Army, David Breeze
Roman Britain, S. J. Hill and S. Ireland
Roman Egypt, Livia Capponi
Roman Frontiers in Britain, David Breeze
The Roman Poetry of Love, Efi Spentzou
Slavery in Classical Greece, N. Fisher
Spectacle in the Roman World, Hazel Dodge
Studying Roman Law, Paul du Plessis

Democracy in Classical Athens

Second Edition

Christopher Carey

BLOOMSBURY ACADEMIC
LONDON • NEW YORK • OXFORD • NEW DELHI • SYDNEY

BLOOMSBURY ACADEMIC
Bloomsbury Publishing Plc
50 Bedford Square, London, WC1B 3DP, UK
1385 Broadway, New York, NY 10018, USA

BLOOMSBURY, BLOOMSBURY ACADEMIC and the Diana logo are trademarks of Bloomsbury Publishing Plc

First published 2000
This edition published 2017
Reprinted 2017 (Twice), 2019

A catalogue record for this book is available from the British Library.

Library of Congress Cataloging-in-Publication Data
Carey, Christopher (Classicist), author.
Democracy in Classical Athens / Christopher Carey.
Second edition. | London; New York: Bloomsbury Academic, an imprint of Bloomsbury Publishing Plc, 2016. | Series: Classical world
Includes bibliographical references.
LCCN 2016027331 (print) | LCCN 2016045730 (ebook) | ISBN 9781474286367 (paperback) | ISBN 9781474286381 (epdf) | ISBN 9781474286374 (epub)
LCSH: Democracy–Greece–Athens. | Athens (Greece)–Politics and government. | BISAC: HISTORY / Ancient / Greece. | POLITICAL SCIENCE / Political Ideologies / Democracy. | RELIGION / Ancient.
LCC JC75.D36 C344 2016 (print) | LCC JC75.D36 (ebook)
DDC 320.938/5–dc23
LC record available at https://lccn.loc.gov/2016027331

ISBN: PB: 978-1-4742-8636-7
ePDF: 978-1-4742-8638-1
eBook: 978-1-4742-8637-4

Series: Classical World

Typeset by RefineCatch Limivted, Bungay, Suffolk
Printed and bound in Great Britain

To find out more about our authors and books visit www.bloomsbury.com and sign up for our newsletters.

Contents

Preface to the First Edition

This book comes with a double health warning. First of all, there is no such thing as a transparent presentation of Athenian democracy. The writer brings an array of prejudices which impact in a variety of ways on the presentation. My own prejudices will be visible enough. Second, the scale of this book has inevitably meant omissions and compressions which give the illusion of firmness to issues which are elusive, uncertain and contentious. I hope that the basic approach adopted will at least allow my readers to get behind my account. Where possible I have used quotations from ancient texts to allow access to the primary sources; otherwise I have incorporated as many references as I could. I hope that any irritation at massed references will be offset by the autonomy they allow the reader. The sources are self-explanatory, the few exceptions are listed in the *Suggested Further Reading* at the end.

My debts to previous scholarship are immense; the most significant (though not the sole) sources are listed in the *Suggested Further Reading*. My thanks are due to Michael Gunningham for his invitation to contribute to the series; writing the book has been far more enjoyable for me than reading it can ever be. I also wish to thank Robin Osborne, who read a first draft and generously took the time to make a number of detailed and invaluable comments; weak or pedestrian points will almost invariably coincide with moments when I have ignored his advice. Finally, my thanks are due to the staff at Bristol Classical Press for turning the word-processed text into a neat volume.

CC

RHUL 1 May 2000

Note to the 2001 Corrected Reprint

In preparing this corrected edition I have taken the opportunity to remove typographical errors (all mine) and adjust some points of detail. The corrections owe much to an in-flight transatlantic reading by Paul Cartledge, for whose careful comments I am profoundly grateful.

CC

RHUL July 2001

Preface to the Second Edition

I am grateful to Alice Wright for her suggestion of a second edition, which has allowed me to update the discussion on some points, and to the generosity of the press readers, who offered detailed and helpful criticism and suggestions for change. I have taken up as many of their suggestions as I could and probably should have taken up more. The changes immediately visible are the addition of a chapter on religion and the expansion of the chapter on the material remains. The first of these fills a gap noted in the original edition and rightly picked up by one or two reviewers. The addition to the material remains was prompted in the first instance by the rewarding experience of teaching on the stimulating 'Athens and Attica' course at Royal Holloway with Lene Rubinstein and Jari Pakkenen. Some of the revised content has already appeared in the excellent Greek translation of the book by Eleni Volonaki of the University of the Peloponnese at Kalamata. Once again I must stress the enormous enjoyment which the writing has given me; a poor excuse for foisting the book once more on readers who have done me no harm but it will have to serve. In particular I have appreciated the opportunity to revisit the continuing scholarship on Athenian democracy. I hope I give due credit in the annotated bibliography at the close. All dates in the book are BC unless otherwise specified.

CC

UCL March 2016

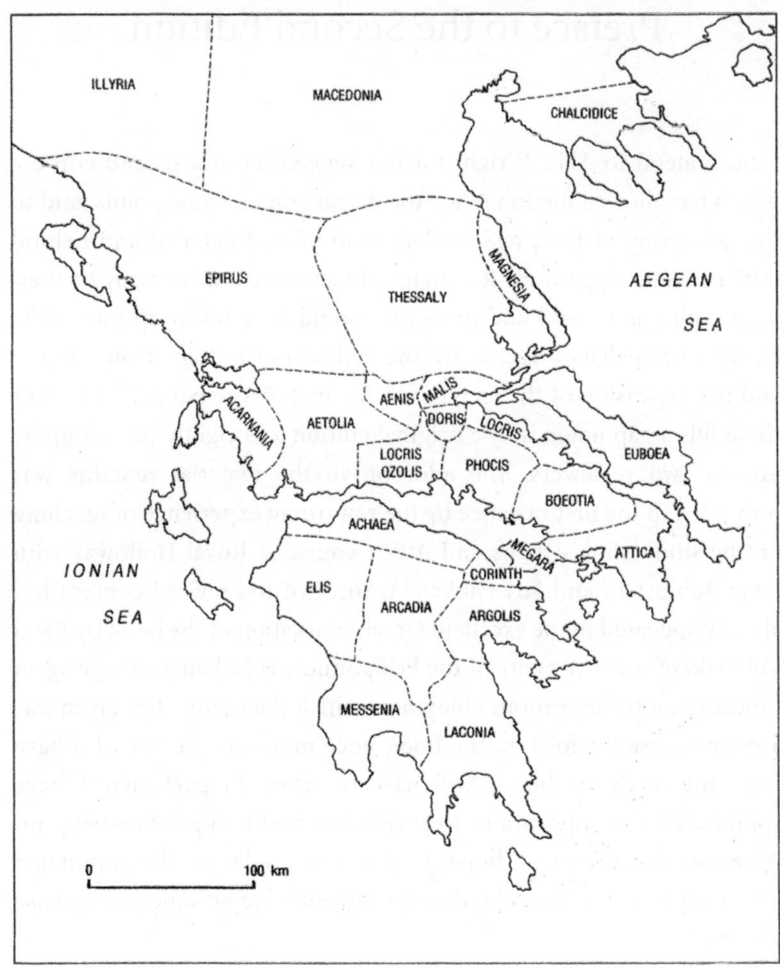

Figure 0.1 Map of Greece.

Figure 0.2 Attica.

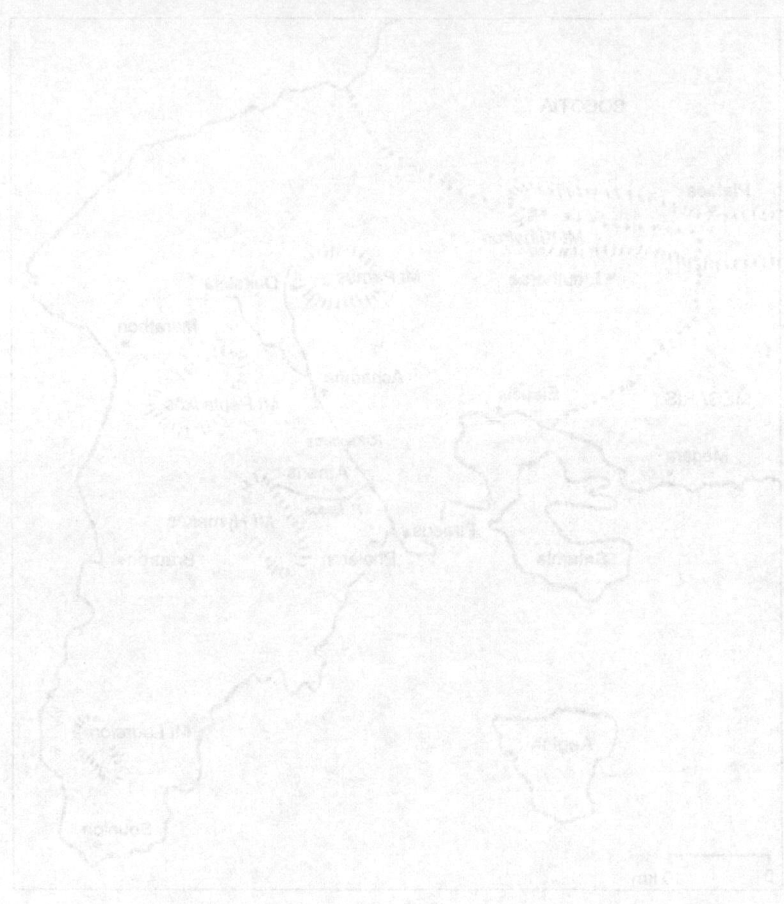

1

First Thoughts

1.1. Defining democracy

The English term 'democracy' is defined by the *Oxford English Dictionary* as 'government by the people', yet there is no single template for democracy in the modern world. Even if we exclude systems whose claim to democratic status is fraudulent or suspect, contemporary democracies differ widely both in the degree of direct popular control of different aspects of the political process and in the mechanisms by which this control is exercised.

The Greek word *demokratia*, 'rule/power/control by/of the *demos*', is as broad as the English term. The word 'demos' is used with two meanings. It can refer to the population as a whole (English 'people') or it can refer to the majority ('the masses') as distinct from a more privileged group. *Demokratia* always describes a political structure in which power is broadly distributed, though the breadth of distribution varies. It is distinguished on the one hand from constitutions in which power is exercised by a single individual, (*basileia* or *tyrannis*, that is traditional kingship or dictatorship, though usage of the terms is fluid) and those in which power is confined to an elite group (*aristokratia* or *oligarchia*). The tripartite division goes back at least to the first quarter of the fifth century. In his *Second Pythian*, probably in the 470s, Pindar lists three kinds of political system: aristocracy ('when the wise watch over the city'); *tyrannis;* and third 'when the noisy host, *ho labros stratos*, [watches over the city]'.[1] The terminology of *demokratia* is first attested explicitly in Herodotos and Aristophanes, the former probably and the latter certainly in the 420s.[2] But it can be pushed back to the 460s at least in the description of democratic Argos in Aischylos' *Suppliant*

Women. Popular sovereignty in the Assembly is described there with the words 'the controlling/governing [*kratousa*] vote of the people [*demos*]',[3] which looks like an etymology of *demokratia*. Aischylos' Argos there behaves very like Athens, from the accountability of the king to the demos (like an Athenian public official) through to the operation of the Assembly (600–614):

> Danaos: Be confident, my children. All is well with the inhabitants.
> The people's sovereign decrees have been decided.
> Chorus: Welcome, old man, who bring news most dear to me.
> Tell us, how is the result decided?
> Which way does the ruling hand of the people prevail?
> Danaos: The Argives decided in no uncertain terms
> but so that my aged mind regains its youth.
> For with favouring hands all together
> the air bristled as they ratified these words:
> that we may live as metics in this land in freedom
> subject to no seizure and in security from all men.
> And no local or outsider may arrest us.
> If any force is brought to bear,
> Any inhabitant who fails to give aid
> is rightless and subject to exile imposed by the people.

Even the language of the decision (*edoxen Argeiois*, 'the Argives decided') resembles that of Athenian democratic decrees (*edoxe toi demoi*, 'the *demos* decided'). The parallel strongly suggests (though it cannot prove) that the Athenians had begun to call their constitution *demokratia* by this time at least. It has been suggested that the word itself is originally pejorative but (even though democracy always had its critics, starting with Pindar) the evidence for this is limited.

Aristotle in the *Politics* (1317b17ff.) observes:

> The following are the features of democracy. That all offices are filled from the whole population. That the mass rules the individual and each individual rules the mass in turn. That the offices are filled by lot, or the ones which do not require experience or skill. That office is not based on property requirement, or a minimal one. That the same man

> may not hold any office twice, or only a few times, with few exceptions, apart from those connected with war. That either offices are held for a short duration in all cases or wherever possible. That all from the whole population may serve as jurors on all matters or on most, and on the most important and decisive . . . [T]hat the Assembly has absolute power while no office has power on any issue or only in very minor ones, or the Council has power on the most important issues (the Council is the most democratic office . . .). Then again that ideally all receive pay, Assembly, courts, offices, or failing that the offices, the courts, the Council and the main assembly meetings, or those offices which must dine together . . .

Aristotle is here identifying the essential features of *demokratia*. Not all of these features applied to every constitution that went by the name. Hence the constant stream of alternatives as he allows for different kinds of *demokratia*. Elsewhere[4] Aristotle recognizes more explicitly different types of *demokratia*, defined according to the occupations of those with citizen rights and the degree of direct popular control. Like 'democracy', *demokratia* is a *kind* of political system, rather than a specific structure.

Examples of *demokratia* began to emerge in city-states of the Greek world in the late archaic period. Athens was one of the earliest states to experiment with it. Its version was constantly evolving, at varying rates, from the end of the sixth century to the suppression of democracy in 322. Yet the same terminology is used by observers and participants to define different phases in the evolution of the Athenian constitution. Herodotos describes the constitution set up by Kleisthenes at the end of the sixth century as *demokratia*. Thucydides has Perikles and Kleon, among others, use the term *demokratia* for the more radical democracy of the late fifth century. And writers like Demosthenes and Aischines use the same term to describe the system in operation in the fourth century.[5]

So in studying Athenian *demokratia* we are taking aim at a moving target. In practice, however, the dearth of evidence prevents a detailed study of the functioning of the democracy in the half century after Kleisthenes. So the descriptive sections of this book concentrate in in many respects throughout the classical period, relying on the spoken word in many contexts where we would regard written documentation as inevitable. Even in public life records were limited by modern standards. Though law once enacted was inscribed on stone, the draft copies of legislation placed on public display (when the practice became the norm in the fourth century) were intended to give advance information of proposals for new laws as part of the legislative process; publication was used for immediate and temporary practical purposes and not for permanent record. From the late fifth century onwards, the Athenians had a central collection of laws. But the texts survived in a legislative vacuum. Inscriptions show that precise minutes were taken of decisions and proposers of decrees at meetings of the Assembly, yet no permanent record was kept of the course of political debate. When Thucydides speaks of reconstructing debate in the Assembly, he automatically speaks of the oral testimony of those present, not of public records.[6] So the crucial question of the rationale behind particular pieces of legislation remains a matter for informed conjecture, as it was for the Athenians themselves in later generations.

Other obvious sources of information are also lacking. The practice of publishing political speeches came late, probably not before the fourth century. So we lack the arguments of the proponents of fifth-century constitutional change. Memoirs from public figures are likewise scarce. Thucydides, who must have been politically active in the 420s, gives himself only passing mention in his history of the Peloponnesian War, while Xenophon, who has left us an account of part of his career, was never a significant political figure in Athens.

Perhaps the greatest silence, as for most periods of human history, is that of the ordinary Athenian. We can deduce much about the attitudes of the mass of Athenians from the way speakers in court or in the Assembly address their audience. Creative literature gives us some plausible impersonations of the ordinary man, for instance in the comic heroes of Aristophanes and the bourgeois characters and slaves who frequent the plots of Menander, or in the peasant farmer who speaks in Orestes' defence in the trial in Euripides' *Orestes*. But the voices we hear are all created by members of the elite. The ordinary Athenian male, like the Athenian female of any class, is silent.

So what do we have?

1.2.1 Inscriptions

Though inscriptions on stone appear in Greece from the seventh century, inscriptions from the seventh century itself are few. They become more frequent in Attica during the sixth century and increase dramatically from the middle of the fifth century, in the wake of the emergence of the empire and the creation of the full democracy. The inscriptions provide valuable information about the operation of the democracy both at state and at deme level. In this they complement and fill (sometimes major) gaps in the literary sources. At the most basic level, they tell us about the formulae for recording decisions of the people. Sometimes, through the addition of riders to decrees based on amendments to substantive proposals, they give us an insight into the operation of the Assembly. They provide information on the administration of the empire, on the role of public bodies and public officials, sometimes officials unknown from other sources, on matters of finance and public cult, on the operation of subgroups of the democracy such as the demes, and on the relations between the people and their officials. Many decrees, particularly for the fourth century, deal with privileges granted to benefactors of the people and so illuminate not only status distinctions and related rights but also the system of rewards and honours which counted for so much in a society much concerned with public honour. However, the accident of survival leaves serious gaps in our sources and in our knowledge for the classical period and still more so for key stages in the evolution of the constitution in the archaic and early classical period.

1.2.2 History and biography

Fifth- and early fourth-century writers (Herodotos, Thucydides and Xenophon) provide information on the evolution and operation of the

the change in the role of the Areiopagos under the democratic reforms of Ephialtes in the 460s is the *Eumenides* of Aischylos, produced in 458. Though the political amalgam which we find in tragedy is still far removed from the political structures of Athens, tragedy on occasion supplements the limited evidence in Herodotos and Thucydides and allows us to hear echoes of fifth-century discussion of the merits and problems of democracy and ultimately of the arguments used in political debate to pursue and defend constitutional change.

1.2.5 Oratory

Apart from Andokides' speech *On his return* (probably published early in the fourth century), we have no fifth-century political speech. The practice of publishing Assembly speeches arose during the fourth century but, even so, little has survived other than the Assembly speeches of Demosthenes. However, we do have a small number of courtroom speeches, real and fictitious, from the last decade or so of the fifth century. Not surprisingly (given the political importance of the courts), some of these speeches provide information on aspects of democratic politics. The fourth century has given us a more substantial body of courtroom speeches, however. In particular, we have a substantial number of speeches delivered either at political trials or at trials with a political motive. Since speeches delivered in court or in the Assembly might be revised for publication, there is always some uncertainty whether we are reading exactly what the first audience heard. But since it is unlikely that speeches were completely rewritten for publication, we are probably reasonably close to the original text. As with all sources, these speeches must be viewed with caution. Since they were always written to secure a particular result, in court or Assembly, the speaker may distort events, misrepresent individual careers or audience practices in order to bamboozle, conciliate or on occasion provoke the audience. The only constraint is the speaker's perception of what an audience familiar with the events can be made to believe, and even this constraint is absent when the speaker digresses to deal with the distant past. A speaker is on the whole more likely to tell the truth where facts are presented in passing as background information rather than as part of the main thrust of the argument. But even here caution is needed. When Demosthenes and Aischines reconstruct events leading to the Peace of Philokrates of 346 in court three years later, we can already detect distortions; and when they revisit the same events in 330 at a further trial, we find discrepancies between the earlier and later accounts. The same caution is needed in dealing with the political speeches of Isokrates, which were more in the nature of pamphlets than publicly delivered speeches.

But not all speeches were written for the courts and the Assembly. One important class of oratory was *epideictic* oratory, that is, oratory of display. Like all Greeks, the Athenians loved oratory and on certain public occasions grandiloquent speeches were delivered. In Athens the most important occasion for this kind of oratory was the public funerals for the war dead which were held at the end of each year during wartime. Like all ritual these funerals were as much about group identity as about religion and the praise of Athens in funeral orations provides an insight into collective ideology.

Under 'oratory' I also include the poetic fragments of Solon. In the archaic period, poetry supplemented prose as the language of political debate, and (in an age when prose had no artistic status) was the only means of placing political views on permanent record. Fragments of Solon's political poetry are preserved in the *Athenian Constitution* and elsewhere. They are a useful supplement to our meagre accounts of the late seventh and early sixth centuries. But they are Solon's own version of his achievements and their aim is to promote or defend his reforms. Presumably the account will always remain within the bounds of what an audience familiar with the events will (however grudgingly) accept; but this still leaves a lot of room for creative rewriting. The fragments are often unspecific on points of practical detail, which has implications for our reading of sources in and after the classical period which mined Solon for information.

1.2.6 Philosophers

Philosophy in the classical period was never far removed from public affairs. Protagoras[8] claimed to teach his students to manage the household and the city more effectively. The dialogues of Plato present individuals prominent in public life engaging in serious debate on philosophical issues. Sokrates is presented by Plato as vocal in his criticism of Athenian democracy. In the *Republic* Plato sketches out an imaginary constitution and in the process advances criticisms of different types of political system. Although the work is more interested in ethical issues than in practical politics, Plato can claim to be the father of political philosophy. He returned to the subject of constitutional theory in the *Laws*. Sokrates' execution left Plato with a jaundiced view of Athenian democracy. As a source for the operation of Athenian democracy he is unreliable. But the criticisms of democracy in his works, especially *Protagoras, Gorgias*, and *Republic*, contribute to our knowledge of contemporary constitutional debate, as does the defence of the principles underlying democracy placed in the mouth of Protagoras at *Protagoras* 322c–323a. Plato's pupil Aristotle was deeply interested in political structures. He and his own pupils compiled a large corpus of accounts of the constitutions of Greek states; the *Athenian Constitution (Athenaion Politeia)*, already mentioned, remains an invaluable source for Athenian political and constitutional history. Aristotle's more general political treatise, *Politics*, draws in part on Athenian experience in its treatment of democracy. Given Aristotle's love of taxonomy, it also helps us more than any other ancient text to identify what for contemporary observers and participants were the essential features of democratic politics. However, though Sokrates played a minor part in politics, both Plato and Aristotle (who was not an Athenian citizen) are viewing politics from the margin.

1.2.7 Lexica

Something has already been said about later sources. But a separate comment is needed on the later lexica, which arose in an age when continuing interest in classical Athens was matched by a narrowing school curriculum and a desire, amid a vast body of literature, to access information in summary form. The lexica present a great deal of detailed information on Athenian political practice, often derived from speeches of the classical period. But even where specific authors are cited, we cannot always be certain that the original has been represented correctly; and where no authority is given we are unsure of the quality of our information.

1.2.8 Archaeology

Archaeological discoveries continue to enhance our understanding of democratic Athens. Archaeological evidence has added greatly to our knowledge of the individual demes. Physical remains tell us much about political space in general in Athens and the history of specific structures. The excavations in the Agora, the administrative and religious heart of the city, and on the Pnyx, where the Assembly met, are particularly important. Recent inscriptional finds and reinterpretation of the remains have led to a fundamental rethink of the physical and political history of the Agora and to significant revisions of the scale of the Theatre of Dionysos. They have also brought to light part of the Demosion Sema, the burial area for the Athenian war dead in the (ancient) suburb of the Kerameikos, as well as pits probably identifiable with the hasty burials in the context of the fifth-century plague. Here the work on the metro system for the 2004 Olympics has proved a very rich source of new finds. At a more basic level archaeological finds can be used to check, and in turn can be checked by, the guidebook to Greece written during the Roman period by the traveller Pausanias, which incorporates a description of Athens. Pottery finds have increased our knowledge of ostracism and in the process have also shed light on the operation of political groups in Athens. In the case of the law courts the excavations have supplemented information available from literary sources about the equipment used.

2

The Road to Democracy

Radical constitutional change is sometimes brought about by revolution, as in France during the eighteenth century or Iran during the twentieth. In these cases the revolution was ideologically driven; a particular set of political ideas, in the one case secular, in the other religious, played a major role in the thinking of the proponents of revolution and in shaping the new political system. Until the oligarchic regimes at the close of the fifth century, there was no Athenian revolution, in the narrow sense of a single coup which overthrew the previous regime. Democracy came into being by a protracted series of giant leaps interspersed with smaller steps, rather than in a single bound. There was a democratic ideology in existence by the middle of the fifth century and this certainly helped to shape the radical democracy of the latter part of the century, but the major constitutional changes of the sixth century were driven more by circumstances than by ideology. Because we read backwards, it is difficult when reviewing the history of the constitution to avoid seeing the radical democracy as the inescapable end result of forces set in motion by Solon. But history is inevitable only in retrospect; different participants or different decisions at critical moments could have produced radically different results. To the participants in the various phases, however, it was anything but inevitable, and for some it was anything but desirable, that Athens would become a democracy.

2.1 Aristocracy in crisis – the seventh century

Our fullest account of the Athenian constitution before Solon comes from the *Athenian Constitution*, Chapters 2–3. The account is condensed and obscure in many aspects of chronology, but it offers a plausible picture of the political system, if only in broad outline. During the seventh century Athens was ruled by an aristocracy. The chief officials, as they were to remain until the fifth century, were the archons, who were selected on the basis of wealth and birth. Their duties included jurisdiction in legal matters. From the account of Solon's reforms in *Athenian Constitution* 7.3, we can be fairly confident that there was already a popular Assembly (*ekklesia*) in the seventh century, though before Solon it excluded the lowest economic group, the *thetes*. It appears to have had little if any formal political power; possibly it functioned as a sounding board for competing views and an arena for aristocratic competition in the manner of the mass agora in the Homeric epics. We have no idea how often or under what circumstances it met. The most significant political force in the state was the Council of the Areiopagos (in the archaic and classical period *Areios pagos*, 'Hill of Ares'), which consisted of ex-archons. Its members held office for life. Its powers included oversight over the laws; it was this body which debated issues of constitution and public policy and which appointed the magistrates.[1]

But in Athens, as elsewhere in Greece in the seventh century, the ruling group found themselves under pressure for change. It is at this period that we find the first tyrannies in Greece. The non-Greek word *tyrannis* was used by the Greeks to designate non-traditional monarchies (what we would call dictatorships), in contrast to *basileia*, 'kingship', the term used for hereditary monarchies. The typical pattern appears to be for a member of the aristocracy to set himself up as dictator, *tyrannos*, by representing himself as champion of the disaffected.

Tyranny was delayed at Athens until the sixth century. But we can discern both evidence for discontent and attempts to stave off radical change with concessions. The term used by the *Athenian Constitution* to describe the constitution at this period is 'oligarchic',[2] and probably political power was confined to a narrow group within the wealthy and well-born. So we should not imagine the disaffected as consisting at this point solely of the poor. Certainly the first attempt to overthrow the regime came from within the ranks of the wealthy. A further force for change was the rise of hoplite warfare with its use of massed lines of heavy-armed infantry, which placed the burden of warfare on those who could provide their own armour; with responsibility for the safety of the state comes a desire for a say in its functioning. Though we have no direct evidence for pressure from this source, the presence of more general hostility toward the existing regime and not merely tensions among the elite can be inferred from Solon's opening of public office beyond the wealthy.

The dissatisfaction among the wealthy may explain changes in the archonship during the seventh century. According to the *Athenian Constitution*[3] the original three archons were supplemented by the addition of six *thesmothetai* (literally 'lawmakers'). Though the date is uncertain, the increase in the number of archons was in place by the last third of the century.[4] The change may have intended to limit the capacity for arbitrary exercise of power by individual archons by expanding the board as a whole.

Whatever the reason for this development, pressure for change remained. In the late 630s or 620s an attempt was made to set up a tyranny.[5] A wealthy Athenian named Kylon attempted to seize the Acropolis and set himself up as tyrant, with the support of his father-in-law, Theagenes, the tyrant of Megara. The attempt was miscalculated. The Athenians rallied together to put down the coup and many of the insurgents were subsequently massacred. Either dissatisfaction was not sufficiently widespread by the last third of the century to commit large numbers of the population to revolutionary change or Kylon's use of foreign troops created a suspicion that his aim was to make Athens a puppet state of Megara.

If the panic reaction of the massacre of the Kylonians reflects insecurity within the oligarchic regime, those in power still recognized the need for concessions to the disaffected. In 621/620[6] Drakon was appointed to write down the laws, which were published on numbered *axones*, probably rotating drums of wood. Of Drakon himself we know nothing. Even his existence has been doubted; and it has been rightly observed that the narrative of a single author of a written law code is both a commonplace in the Greek world and suspiciously close to the Greek tendency to look for a 'first inventor' (*protos heuretes*). But the historicity of Drakon is less important than the date, which fits into a verifiable trend (we can substitute a committee without affecting the narrative). There is tendency in Greece at this period to inscribe the laws, probably in response to the widespread pressure for change. It is impossible to determine how many Athenians could read (at whatever level of literacy) at this period. Some certainly could and presumably many people with little or no claim to literacy could access the laws through an intermediary. But the public inscription of the laws is not only about consultation: there is enormous symbolic importance in the removal of knowledge of the law from a narrow group of magistrates and its location in public space where it becomes available to the whole population. It is unlikely that Drakon made any change to the constitution. In fact, it is questionable whether he actually drafted new laws rather than inscribing existing practice. Later tradition made Drakon's laws unusually harsh but this is probably assumption based on the recodification by Solon and on Solon's reputation as the founder of democracy, as well as Solon's own tendency to present Athens before and after his reforms as dystopia yielding place to order and justice.

2.2 Solon's reforms

Drakon's intervention may have delayed but it did not stop the pressure for change, which was compounded by economic crisis. It is impossible to reconstruct the crisis which Solon faced with any confidence and there is scarcely any detail which is not subject to controversy. We are left with the trenchant account of the *Athenian Constitution* (Chapter 2) supplemented by additional detail from Plutarch's *Solon*, though Plutarch is often himself using the *Athenian Constitution* or its sources. For some issues we have Solon's own words but Solon is more interested in the ethical dimension and political impact of his policies than in relating the detail, and the vagueness of his account meant that fourth-century sources disagreed about the nature both of the crisis and of his reforms, as we learn from Plutarch.[7] The picture which emerges from the *Athenian Constitution* and Plutarch is that 'the poor' found themselves in debt to larger landholders. Given the limited role of coinage in the Greek world at this period, presumably these 'loans' would consist of produce. The reason for them is irrecoverable. But the statement of the *Athenian Constitution* that the poor had to work the land of the rich, together with the terminology used to describe them, *hektemoroi* ('sixth-part-men'), suggests that the debt was repayable both in labour and in a share of produce. The *Athenian Constitution* uses the language of slavery (the verb used is *douleuein*, from *doulos*, 'slave') to describe their condition. But the other term it uses of them (with *hektemoroi*) is *pelatai*, which later writers use to translate the Latin word *cliens*, 'client', i.e. a free inferior; this is not literal chattel slavery but a kind of indentured labour. Failure to meet their obligations left them and their families liable to seizure as slaves; some at least were sold abroad.[8] Solon himself claims[9] to have removed the stone markers, *horoi*, from the earth. Traditionally this was taken to indicate a boundary stone placed on the property of smallholders to indicate that the land was security for a debt. This use of the term is not securely attested before the fourth century. This could be chance; but Solon's words could also describe encroachment by the rich on private or common land and on this as in much else about Solon the jury is still out.

Regardless of the difficulty of extracting a detailed account, we can accept with confidence the summation of the *Athenian Constitution*[10] that the poor 'had no share in anything', that is, they had neither wealth nor power. It is tempting to see here a sudden crisis; but it could be a slow development. It is even possible that the situation described in *Athenian Constitution* was normal and that the crisis reflects not a change in the economic situation but simply growing impatience among the victims. Restrictive regimes are often at their most vulnerable when they accept the need to change, and it is possible that the concessions made in the preceding decades had merely fuelled the existing dissatisfaction.

By 594/3 the hostility to the ruling elite had brought Athens close to civil war. Solon was elected archon and given the task of mediating between the sides. The *Athenian Constitution*[11] calls Solon 'the first champion of the *demos*', placing him in the same category as later figures such as Perikles and Kleon. Other classical sources echo the depiction of Solon as 'democratic'. But it is unlikely that the ruling group (whose policy had been to make the minimum concessions needed to avert revolution) would have accepted him as mediator if he was perceived as committed to their opponents. Nor in fact does Solon present himself as a partisan of the discontented. In the fragments of his poetry Solon is equally ready to criticize both sides and prides himself on steering a middle course:

> To the people [*demos*] I gave as much privilege as suffices
> neither taking from or adding to its honour [*time*].
> And those who had power and were admired for their wealth,
> for them too I contrived that they should have no dishonour.
> I stood casting my strong shield over both,
> and did not allow either side an unjust victory.
>
> fr.5

Nonetheless, Solon's reforms were wide-ranging, even if they fell short of the demands of the more radical proponents of change. The most important economic measure was the *seisachtheia* ('shaking off of burdens') or cancellation of debts, accompanied by a law forbidding debts incurred on the security of the person. This act had enormous political ramifications beyond the immediate conciliation of the impoverished, since it affected the conceptualization of the native Athenians collectively as a distinct and privileged group.

There were also major changes both in the judicial system and in the corpus of laws. The *Athenian Constitution*[12] famously states that Solon retained only the homicide laws from Drakon (the homicide laws alone were still termed 'Drakon's laws' in the classical period); but probably there was far more continuity between the codes of Drakon and Solon than our sources acknowledge. The laws were placed on display; our sources refer again to *axones*, as with Drakon, but also to *kyrbeis*, perhaps more durable stone pillars.

A major change in the administration of justice was the introduction of the *graphe*, the public action, which allowed anyone to bring a prosecution in certain cases, where previously only the alleged victim (or in cases of homicide, the family) could act. This gave the weak a measure of protection against the strong through the justice system by allowing a potential prosecutor to intervene on behalf of someone who was unable or unwilling to take action on grounds of age, status, financial or social position or gender. In the classical period this meant in practice that when prosecution was not initiated by the aggrieved person, the prosecutor was usually a personal or political enemy of the defendant. Whether this was the original intention is unknowable and probably irrelevant, since the effect was still to open up a means of prosecution on behalf of those who could not act for themselves. The judicial powers of the magistrates were restricted by the creation of a right of appeal (*ephesis*) to a court.[13]

There were also major constitutional changes. The middle-ranking public offices were opened up to the top three property classes: the *pentekosiomedimnoi* ('five hundred bushel men', i.e. those whose land could yield five hundred bushels of dry or liquid produce); the *hippeis* ('cavalry'); and *zeugitai* ('yokemen'). From the fact that we hear of no further change in eligibility for the archonship before the admission of the third class, the *zeugitai*, in 457/6,[14] it is probable (but not certain) that Solon opened the archonship to the top two classes. Though the substitution of economic for birth qualifications for office probably had only limited impact (Athens was not a major trading state at this period and social mobility through new wealth will not have been widespread), the change was of enormous significance in the long term; it introduced flexibility into a closed and fixed political system, creating a path for access to office for those with wealth derived from trade.

The lowest property class, the *thetes* ('labourers') were admitted to the Assembly and to the lawcourts (which at this stage may have been the Assembly sitting in a judicial capacity). We are also told[15] that Solon created a Council of 400, 100 from each of the four Athenian tribes then in existence. If the statement is true, the Council's role was limited, presumably to preparing business for the Assembly, since the Areiopagos retained its traditional role as guardian of the laws and the constitution, with powers to supervise and discipline magistrates.[16]

2.3 The sixth-century tyranny

The fragments of Solon indicate that his compromise solution to the political tensions left groups on both sides of the political divide dissatisfied. The two decades after Solon's archonship saw a continuation of the political struggle. There were years when no archon was selected (*Athenian Constitution* uses the term *anarchia*, 'anarchy', i.e. absence of the office of archon[17]) and there was an attempt by one archon, Damasias, to prolong his office into something like a tyranny. The sources give the political divisions a geographical dimension, with the population divided into three groups: the 'Plainsmen' (i.e. from the central plain of Attica) under Lykourgos; the 'Coastmen' under the Alkmaionid Megakles, a descendant of the archon who executed the supporters of Kylon; and 'The men beyond the hills' (from east Attica), led by Peisistratos.[18] Peisistratos' own career illustrates the political instability in Athens at this period, for he was first tyrant and then exile twice, as alliances shifted between the political factions, before he finally consolidated his power in 546/5.[19]

Peisistratos appears to have left the Solonian constitution intact. He maintained his power not by any formal consolidation of his authority but by manipulating the selection of the magistrates,[20] and by forging alliances with powerful families, as we can see from the archon lists for the 520s, where members of Peisistratos' family appear alongside members of the great Athenian families of the period. The term 'tyrant' summons up images of brutal oppression. But the Greek terms *tyrannos* and *tyrannis* merely define an autocracy as non-constitutional in origin. It was only later that the term *tyrannos* came to mean 'tyrant' in our sense. The rule of Peisistratos appears to have been moderate.

Greek tyrannies rarely survived beyond the second generation, and the Athenian sixth-century tyranny is no exception. Peisistratos was succeeded on his death in 528/7 by his three sons. One of these, Hipparchos, was murdered by Harmodios and Aristogeiton in 514 in a debacle which nonetheless earned them a place in Athenian political legend as martyrs for freedom. Thrown on to the defensive, the regime became more oppressive and was finally overthrown in 510 with Spartan aid.

The Peisistratid tyranny could be mistaken for a pause in the evolution of the Athenian constitution. In fact it was a vital part of that evolution. After Peisistratos' second restoration, the tyranny provided Athens with three decades of political stability. By allowing time for the consolidation of the constitutional arrangements of Solon, it made a return to oligarchy more difficult. It was at this period that Athens gained territory on both sides of the entrance to the Black Sea, thus pointing forward to the imperial role of the fifth century, while the status of Athens as leading city of the Ionian Greeks was established. Within Athens itself, the reorganization of state festivals, especially the Panathenaia and the City Dionysia, offered a counterweight to the geographical divisions which had inflamed political rivalry and pointed forward to the reforms of the new democracy at the end of the century. In the case of Peisistratos himself this centralizing process was reinforced by personal visits to different parts of the territory and by the appointment of itinerant 'deme judges' (*dikastai kata demous*) to resolves disputes in the countryside,[21] reducing the scope for local patronage and interference from the elite. The *Athenian Constitution* claims[22] that Peisistratos also advanced loans to farmers, which if true represents an attempt both to alleviate continuing rural poverty and to substitute central for local patronage.

2.4 The reforms of Kleisthenes

According to our sources, the next constitutional leap came about not from ideology but from political pragmatism.[23] The fall of the tyranny, brought about with the support of Sparta,[24] was followed by a fresh struggle for power, this time between Isagoras and the Alkmaionid Kleisthenes. To counteract Isagoras' power base within the aristocracy, Kleisthenes appealed to the masses for support. The sources use the language of political factions to describe the power base of the two sides: (*Athenian Constitution*) 'when he was being worsted by the factional clubs/in the factional struggle (*hetaireiai*), Kleisthenes brought the *demos* on to his side'; (Herodotos) 'when he was getting the worst of it Kleisthenes brought the demos into his faction/made the demos his collaborators (*prosetairizetai*)'. The language (together with the insistence that he acted to reverse his inferior position) presents Kleisthenes as a democrat by need and calculation, not by conviction. There is no good reason to doubt this account. But it is not the whole story. Increasing the power of the masses was a means of consolidating Kleisthenes' own position. But it also provided a base for his reforms. Since a visible goal of those reforms was political stability, it is unlikely he would have given the demos a more central role, if he had perceived it as a force for instability. This is pragmatism, not cynicism. The support of the demos enabled him to introduce radical reforms during the very year (508/7) when Isagoras' supremacy in terms of traditional sources of power was reflected in his election as archon.[25]

These reforms irrevocably reshaped the political system. At a single stroke Kleisthenes broke two power bases which had sustained the factional struggles after Solon. The four Ionian tribes of Attica, through which the aristocrats had exercised influence, were replaced by ten new tribes. Kleisthenes also loosened the local allegiances which had formed the nucleus of the factions in the period leading up to the tyranny by dividing Attica into three areas – city, inland and coast – and mixing *demoi*, 'demes' (urban districts or rural villages), from all three to create the new tribes. These new tribes were to form the basis for the selection of a number of officials and for the organization of the citizen army. The subdivisions of the old tribes, the *gene* (aristocratic clans) and the *phratriai* ('brotherhoods') were left in place – they continued to play an important social and religious role throughout the classical period –

but the basis of citizenship from now on was the deme, the smallest formal subdivision of the state. Though Solon has been credited on occasion with the invention of the Athenian citizen, Kleisthenes' fundamental redirection of individual loyalty through the deme to the city gives him at least as good a claim. Kleisthenes also admitted a large number of non-citizens to the demes, and thus to citizen rights,[26] effectively enfranchising as many free inhabitants of Attica as possible and in the process ensuring maximum support for the new system.

He created a Council of 500 (fifty from each tribe); it is not clear whether this was a new foundation or a reorganization of a Solonian Council of 400. The powers of the Kleisthenic Council are nowhere spelled out for us; but probably its main (perhaps its sole) role was to prepare business for the Assembly.

Our information on the Assembly under the Kleisthenic system is sketchy. We have a late fifth-century inscription[27] restricting the power of the Council and defining certain key powers of the Assembly. The presence of archaic language has been taken to indicate that the inscription in part copies an original enacting the Kleisthenic provisions. Unfortunately, alternative dates for the original are possible. But the use of the term *demokratia* for Athens after Kleisthenes (whether or not this was the official term for the constitution at the time) indicates that the Assembly must have had the final say on major issues of public policy. However, the Areiopagos, composed of aristocratic ex-archons, still retained its old functions as guardian of the laws and overseer of the public officials.

Two more measures attributed to Kleisthenes deserve mention. A board of ten generals (*strategoi*) was created,[28] one from each of the ten new tribes. The Polemarchos retained overall command in war. The generals eventually became the most important public officials in the fifth century. The other measure is ostracism, under which the individual who received the largest number of votes at a specially designated Assembly meeting was exiled for ten years; this is described in greater detail later (5.6). If our sources are correct to ascribe the creation of ostracism to Kleisthenes, it remains a puzzle that it was not used until the 480s. But its introduction is consistent with Kleisthenes' overall drive for political cohesion, since it offered a means of averting factional strife by the crude but effective device of decapitating a faction.

The Kleisthenic reforms were cemented in place by heavy-handed intervention by Sparta. In 508/7 the Spartan king Kleomenes, who had earlier intervened to put down the tyranny, invaded Attica in support of Isagoras but was compelled to surrender after being besieged on the Acropolis for two days, thus depriving the opponents of reform simultaneously of military support and legitimacy; a second invasion in 506 crumbled away, providing the newly reshaped Athens with its first major success.[29] A further test came at in 490. Following a common pattern in the late sixth and early fifth centuries, the ousted Peisistratidai appealed to Persia for support and the former tyrant Hippias was with the Persian invaders at Marathon.[30] The Persian defeat put an end to any chance of a restoration of the tyranny, even if it only temporarily checked Persian ambitions. There was no direct link between democracy and military success but the defeat of the old regime, backed by an invasion force from the largest power in the region, must have reinforced collective confidence in the new politics.

2.5 The 460s and after

The first few decades of the fifth century saw a steady consolidation of the system put in place by Kleisthenes. In 487/6, selection by lot replaced election of the nine archons.[31] Though the random selection was still made from a pre-elected shortlist, the change was important, since it significantly reduced the prospects for aristocratic control over the outcome. The consolidation of the power of the demos can also be seen in the use of the ostracism in the context of political competition in the same decade.

The next major constitutional change was initiated in 462/1 by a group led by Ephialtes which included the young Perikles.[32] Previous reforms had left the Areiopagos untouched. But as the democracy grew in confidence, the existence of a powerful body which was not collectively answerable to the people must have seemed increasingly anomalous. Our sources claim that the influence of the Areiopagos had increased in the period after the Persian invasion of 480–479.[33] The statement may be a fourth-century invention, though we lack the means to prove or disprove it. We are told that political charges were brought against individual members of the Areiopagos, while the Areiopagos as a whole was stripped of its political powers and left with jurisdiction in a number of religious areas, principally homicide trials. Some of its judicial powers were given to the Council, others to the Assembly and the courts. We can still catch echoes of the propaganda used by the democrats to substantiate their case; the statement in *Athenian Constitution*[34] that the Areiopagos was stripped of its 'extra/additional powers' (*ta epitheta*) seems to reflect a claim that the traditional powers of the Areiopagos were not part of its (supposed) original functions.

Recent scholarship has questioned the significance of these reforms and suggested that the there is greater continuity between the periods before and after Ephialtes than the fourth-century accounts suggest. Certainly the power of the demos was already considerable, as we can see both from its punishment of leaders who failed it such as Miltiades in the 480s[35] and the fact that Ephialtes could use trials in the Assembly or the popular courts to break the hold of the Areiopagos. But we should not underrate the significance of the reforms for the entrenchment of popular power or the strength of the resistance to the change. The need for the prosecutions itself suggests both that the Areiopagos was like any elite body hostile to any attempt to shrink its influence and also that it was a powerful adversary. The opponents of democracy were also ready to resort to violent and subversive measures. Ephialtes was assassinated. And a group of disaffected aristocrats conspired to betray the city to a Spartan force based in Boiotia in 457 specifically to put down the democracy,[36] a move prefigured by Isagoras in his struggle against Kleisthenes and repeated half a century later when the oligarchic coup of 411 crumbled. But the threat of Spartan invasion was blocked and the fabric of the state held. We have indirect testimony to the anxieties of this period in Aischylos' *Eumenides* of 458, which enacts in mythical form the creation of the Areiopagos as a homicide court. Given its date, the theme was politically loaded. Though scholars are divided on Aischylos' own position, it is difficult to avoid the conclusion that the references to the danger of civil war in the play are inspired by contemporary fears.

The work of Ephialtes was reinforced by a series of measures. The third property class, the *zeugitai*, were admitted to the archonship in 457/6.[37] In the same period pay was introduced for public office and for service on juries. The first of these measures reduced the obstacles which deterred men of more moderate means from seeking office; the second was more significant, given the political role of the courts, since it opened up jury service to all classes, while ensuring an adequate supply of jurors for the increased business of the courts in the wake of Ephialtes' reforms.

2.6 Democracy, navy and empire

So far I have focused on constitutional developments within Athens. But they did not take place in a vacuum. To understand the advance of democracy, we have to locate internal politics in the wider context of the Persian invasions of 490 and 480–479 and their aftermath. For Herodotos (5.78), victory against Persia proved the value of Athenian democracy, and many Athenians must have had their confidence in the post-Kleisthenic system confirmed or inspired by the military successes. But there was another, still more important, aspect to this success, the role of the navy. Scholars have rightly stressed that there is no inevitable link between naval power and democracy; not all naval powers were democracies and not all democracies were naval powers. But in Athens' case, the link is inescapable. In the 480s the Athenians had embarked on the creation of the most powerful navy in Greece under the influence of Themistokles. In the wake of the defeat of the second Persian invasion of 480–479, the Athenians assumed the leadership of a confederacy, the Delian League, which was devoted to following up the Greek success by liberating the Greek cities of Asia Minor (modern Turkey) and the coastal islands from Persian control. By degrees this confederacy was turned into an Athenian empire. It was the navy which brought victory at Salamis, which offered Athens the means to take the offensive against Persia after the war, and on which the city depended for its control over the empire. The fleet required a vast manpower to function and even though we know that non-citizens and even (especially at times of crisis) slaves served in substantial numbers (at least later in the century), the fleet was always heavily reliant on citizen rowers. And the citizens who rowed were those who could not afford either to maintain a horse or to purchase heavy armour for infantry service. There was a tendency in ancient Greece for political power to reflect military importance. Just as the hoplites who bore the brunt of land warfare from the archaic period onward pressed throughout Greece for admission to power, so as the navy became the basis of Athenian power, the poorer citizens pressed for a greater share in the political process. The point is made succinctly by the Old Oligarch:

> First of all I shall say this, that <it seems> right that there [that is, in Athens] <the base> and the poor and the people have the advantage over the noble and the rich, for the following reason. It is the people that rows the ships and confers power on the city, and the helmsmen, the boatswains, the naval under-officers, the prowmen, and the shipwrights – these are the ones who confer power on the city rather than the hoplites, the noble and the decent.
>
> [Xenophon] *Athenian Constitution* 1.2

The connection between democracy and empire went further. As part of the consolidation of power, Athens insisted that all capital cases from the cities of the empire be tried in Athens. This increased the role of the mass juries as an arm of government. The need for a large bureaucratic infrastructure to administer the empire greatly expanded the opportunities for office-holding, a source both of income and of political experience.

Equally important were the broader economic benefits of empire. Except for a small number of states which maintained their nominal independence and provided ships to serve alongside the Athenian fleet, the cities of the empire paid an annual tribute. There was also a substantial indirect income from the empire, for instance in terms of duties on the massive amounts of goods now coming into Peiraeus and the court dues paid by the allies in the wake of the transfer of capital cases from the empire to Athens. The income from the empire was not absolutely necessary to sustain pay for office and for jury service, since (as is often pointed out) the system survived the loss of the empire at the end of the fifth century and was even extended. But as well as helping to finance an ambitious building policy, which both reflected Athens' new status and provided a programme of paid public work, the empire augmented the state income from internal sources and created the financial confidence needed for the introduction of state pay on an unprecedented scale.

2.7 The intellectual climate

The Athenian democracy cannot be fully understood without reference to the intellectual climate within which it and other democracies evolved. The sixth and fifth centuries in Greece were a period of rapid intellectual change, beginning with the Ionian physicists in the sixth century and culminating in the fifth with the activity of the sophists, travelling teachers who found in Athens a favourable environment for their courses on language and rhetoric and their speculations on the world, physical, social and political. Apart from its (often iconoclastic) content, the teaching of the sophists was fundamentally revolutionary in the sense that they were proposing to teach *arete*, 'virtue', 'excellence'. This agenda was diametrically opposed to the traditional aristocratic claim to exclusive possession of this complex combination of social, moral and intellectual superiority. The idea of formal instruction was also alien to the aristocratic approach, which favoured learning by example from older members of one's social class. The proposition that anybody could in theory acquire *arete* both gave momentum to and was in turn given further momentum by the egalitarian tendency of Athenian democracy.

2.8 The new men

There is one last development in the fifth-century democracy to note. This is not a structural change but rather a shift in the social background of the political leaders. Athenian political leaders even under the democracy had traditionally come from old families whose wealth was primarily in land; political activity was an aristocratic competition sponsored by the demos. It remained an elite competition but by the last third of the fifth century we see a change in the political leadership. In general the most influential political leaders in the late fifth century – Kleon, Hyperbolos, Kleophon – came from a non-landed background; and this persists in the fourth century with politicians like Demosthenes. These were still rich men, but their money came from the manufacture (through slave labour) and sale of goods, and their family wealth was of recent origin. Our sources exaggerate the scale and pace of the change. The emergence of the overtly populist Kleon as successor to the aristocratic and aloof Perikles, together with the mockery of the social origins of subsequent political figures by the comic poets, makes the change in leadership patterns seem like a sudden rupture. And this impression is compounded by Thucydides' blanket dismissal of the politicians of the 420s and after,[38] as lacking Perikles' natural superiority and 'more on the same level as each other' (though in fact he is speaking about influence and ability rather than social or economic background). But the process began earlier than our sources suggest. Nikias, born about 470, owed much of his wealth to the silver mines and Kleon too (it has been observed) was already an active and prominent politician in the 430s before Perikles' death, not a sudden arrival in the 420s. The wealth is also only relatively new, at least in some cases; these are not necessarily first generation *nouveaux riches*. Kleon's father Kleainetos was rich enough to have served as *choregos* in the 460s[39] and Kleophon's father had been a general in the early 420s. And the aristocrats did not disappear – Alkibiades, for instance, like Perikles was descended on his mother's side from the Alkmaionidai, who had been prominent under the seventh-century regime. Furthermore, though the old dynasties ceased to provide the political leaders in the fourth century, we still find exceptions, as with the politician Lykourgos, prominent in the late fourth century, who belonged to the distinguished *genos* of Eteoboutadai.

So the shift was longer, slower and less absolute than our sources suggest. But change there was, and the death of the aristocratic Perikles, especially after such a long period of political prominence, must have made it seem more abrupt to contemporary observers. The change in the political leadership reflects larger changes in Athenian society arising from increased opportunities for wealth creation, especially those created directly and indirectly by empire. But one factor in the shift may be the nature of the political process itself. The need to manage a large empire made financial expertise an important qualification for political influence (Perikles owed part of his authority to his financial ability); and the scale and relative complexity of their money-making activity meant that men from a commercial background were more likely to possess it than those whose income came from land.

The sense of rupture was exacerbated by political style. Thucydides in book 3 of his *History* presents Kleon, Perikles' successor, as the dominant figure on the Pnyx, as calculatedly adopting the stance of the simple, uneducated man as a means of positioning himself as an outsider rather than just another politician. Aristophanes suggests that this ostentatious, bluff simplicity was characteristic of the current public speakers:

> Your only weakness is that you read a bit and badly.
> Demagoguery is not the job of an educated man
> these days or one of good character;
> it belongs to the ignorant and the vile.
>
> *Knights* 190–93

Aristophanes also characterizes Kleon's debating manner as coarse, bullying and violent,[40] a picture shared with Thucydides. The *Athenian*

Constitution adds the interesting detail that Kleon was the first politician to shout abuse and hitch up his robe (for vigorous movement) on the rostrum.[41] We cannot really accept the view that Kleon's predecessors had been entirely decorous, not least because of the sheer physical demands of open-air oratory on the Pnyx and the fiercely combative nature of Athenian politics, which did not start with the Peloponnesian War. But probably Kleon did bring a new degree of bluntness, and a more consistently aggressive style and manner, to the rostrum. And he was followed by some at least of his successors. Kleophon, prominent in the final decade of the fifth century, is presented as adopting a violently aggressive manner in the Assembly.[42] The source is biased in the extreme. But even sympathetic sources seem embarrassed by Kleophon;[43] so we can probably accept that his manner was very abrasive.

The comic poets relentlessly mock Perikles' successors for their background, representing them as coarse, uneducated and (with typical comic distortion) of servile origin. It is comedy's job to mock and in part this is just a stick with which to beat those with power, as the comic poets had mocked Perikles relentlessly for the odd shape of his head. But this may not be all. Since the comic poets tend to ride rather than create the waves in public opinion, their criticisms may reflect anxieties among at least some of the audience. The political and rhetorical style of people like Kleon offered one ground for anxiety. Yet the Athenians maintained a respect for birth throughout the history of the democracy and comedy may be reflecting a shared concern at the transfer of political influence to men of obscure origins, even if the Athenians collectively were aware that they needed their expertise.

2.9 Oligarchic interludes I: The Four Hundred

By the time Aristophanes wrote his first plays in the 420s, the radical democracy was firmly in place. Though it had its critics, the constitution had delivered power, prestige and economic growth, and aristocrats were happy enough to participate in its success. This did not preclude insecurity on the part of the demos. Late fifth-century sources indicate a widespread, though probably intermittent, fear of another tyranny. The following passage from Aristophanes' *Wasps* gives some flavour of the Athenian anxieties:

> Everything's tyranny and conspirators as far as you're concerned,
> whether the accusation's something big or something small,
> though I've not even heard the word tyranny, not for fifty years.
> But now it's much cheaper than dried fish,
> so in fact the term is all around the Agora.
>
> 488–92

Though the picture is exaggerated, it is not invented; it finds an echo in Thucydides' account of suspicions arising from the mutilation of the Herms in 415, when the Athenians were as ready to smell tyranny as oligarchy.[44] Ironically the demos was looking in the wrong direction, at least in part. The real danger was from oligarchy. The war against Sparta, fought from 431 to 404 with intermissions, was bound to cause some dissatisfaction, since the financial burdens of war fell upon the rich. But since war also offered them opportunities for military and political advancement, as long as the war seemed winnable the danger of subversion was limited. The fact that individuals prominent in the oligarchies of the last decade had been active in democratic politics indicates that any ideological reservations about democracy were counterbalanced by a pragmatic recognition of the tangible successes of the radical democracy and the benefits to the elite of participation.

The situation changed after the destruction of the expedition sent by Athens to conquer Syracuse in Sicily in 415–413. As an emergency measure the Athenians elected a board of ten, the *probouloi*, to handle the daily business of the city in place of the Council of 500. But there were factions within the city who believed that the democracy was incapable of managing the war against Sparta. When widespread revolt broke out among the subject cities of the empire the people were persuaded in 411 to vote the radical democracy out of existence in the mistaken belief, fostered by Alkibiades, that this would induce Persia to transfer its support from Sparta to Athens. The constitutional change was assisted by a climate of fear generated by a number of assassinations. Under the new constitution power would reside with an Assembly of 5,000; pending the selection of the Five Thousand an interim council of Four Hundred would run the state. Political rights were to be based on property,[45] essentially those of hoplite status and above. All pay for office was terminated.

The oligarchy was fundamentally flawed. With no living experience of non-democratic politics in Athens, the revolutionaries had no consistent ideology and were divided from the start between the moderates who favoured a restricted democracy and the extremists who favoured a narrow oligarchy. This fragile alliance fractured when the fleet at Samos refused to recognize the Four Hundred. The extremists turned to Sparta for support and were overthrown under the influence of the leading moderate, Theramenes. The Four Hundred were replaced by the Five Thousand. Thucydides speaks warmly of the constitution at this period[46] (though he had only second-hand knowledge, since he was in exile at the time) but it did not last and was probably intended as no more than an interim measure; democracy was restored in 410.

2.10 Oligarchic interludes II: The Thirty

Oligarchy experienced a final spasm after the Athenian surrender to Sparta in 404. One of the conditions of surrender was that all exiles should be recalled. These included Kritias, who became the dominant figure in the brutal regime of the Thirty, set up with support from the Spartan commander Lysander. Under the slogan of restoring 'the ancestral constitution' (*patrios politeia*), they reversed the reforms of Ephialtes.[47] But though the regime began with a semblance of moderation, it rapidly degenerated. The mass executions and appropriations of property drove large numbers into exile. Like the earlier oligarchic revolutionaries, the Thirty were divided between the extremists led by Kritias and the moderates led by Theramenes. This

legislative procedures under the restored democracy suggest that there was a collective conviction that the legislative procedures in place in the latter part of the fifth century created the risk of contradiction and confusion. The attempt to remove or avert contradiction is a recurrent feature in Athenian statutes concerning legislation in the fourth century.[50]

But we should not overstate the changes introduced at the restoration. The *Athenian Constitution*[51] rightly notes that the period after 403 showed a steady consolidation of the power of the masses. Some central features of the fifth-century democracy were retained in their entirety. What did not change was the central role of the Assembly in determining state policy. Evidently it was felt that the defeat in the war was not the result of structural flaws in the democracy. The Athenians collectively tended to ascribe bad decisions by the Assembly to bad advice by political figures rather than error by the demos, a tendency perhaps most visible at the opening of book 8 of Thucydides, where after the disaster in Sicily the Athenians turned on all the proponents of the expedition. This tendency was actively encouraged by politicians, who in their struggle for influence regularly attributed bad policy to malice or corruption on the part of their opponents. The essential wisdom of the demos remained unquestioned. In fact, after the restoration the Athenians took a more radical step than any which had been made in the fifth century in introducing pay for attendance at the Assembly.[52]

The consolidation of the power of the masses was also continued in areas such as the procedures for vetting candidates for office, where the role of the lawcourts was expanded. By the time of the composition of the *Athenian Constitution* in the 320s, the process had been taken further; the courts now played an administrative role in allocating important religious (and possibly secular) contracts.[53]

At the same time, and somewhat surprisingly, the Areiopagos experienced a revival. The Areiopagos had lost most of its powers under the reforms of Ephialtes and for the rest of the fifth century it is characterized by silence. But under the revision of the laws in 403/2 the Areiopagos was given the role of ensuring that the magistrates complied with the laws.[54] This was a watching brief only, without significant punitive powers; and sixty years later it still had the power to impose only minor fines.[55] But from the mid-fourth century we can see a gradual increase in its powers. Its responsibility in the area of religion was enhanced when it was given a role in supervising sanctuaries in 352/1.[56] In the 340s it was allowed to investigate and report on political offences, either on its own initiative or at the instruction of the Assembly, under the procedure known as *apophasis*.[57] The Areiopagos could give a preliminary verdict but the Assembly determined the final judgment and punishment.[58] The Areiopagos played an important role in maintaining public order in the emergency after the defeat at Chaironeia in 338.

The accommodation between the democracy and the central body of the pre-democratic state is at first sight surprising. However, the role it was given immediately after the restoration is consistent with the general desire to hedge the constitution round with safeguards. The move shows astute pragmatism on the part of the demos, since the inclusion of the oldest public body in the state more firmly within the democratic structures at one stroke gave the Areiopagos a reason to support the democracy and blunted the rhetorical appeal of potential anti-democratic claims to restore the 'ancestral constitution'. Furthermore, although the Thirty had restored the old powers of the Areiopagos, their main political ally had been not the Areiopagos but the Council of 500. But it took another sixty years for the Athenians to give the Areiopagos a central role in politics and it needed an emergency for them to allow it any substantial punitive powers. The suspicion that the Areiopagos might offer support for a non-democratic coup persisted, as we can see from the law proposed in 337/6 prescribing loss of political rights for any member of the Areiopagos who served under a regime which supplanted the democracy.[59] And still in the 320s it was possible to represent the Areiopagos as having oligarchic leanings.[60]

It is worth pausing at this point to note a striking omission in the progressive consolidation of the power of the demos. The final logical change, the admission of the *thetes* to office, was never officially enshrined in law, though their exclusion had become a dead letter by the fourth century.[61] Other odd but insignificant anomalies remained in place as traces of earlier phases in the evolution of the constitution. The Treasurers of Athena continued to be selected from the *pentekosiomedimnoi* (the highest of Solon's property classes) in the 320s as under Solon's constitution,[62] though the old classification system was no longer meaningful in the economic climate of the fourth century and a member of this tax class might be poor enough to have to supplement his farming with paid work. The Athenians were not interested in constitutional neatness for its own sake.

2.12 Alexander and after

The restored democracy lasted for eight decades. Although Athens never recovered the power it had enjoyed in the fifth century, the early decades of the fourth saw a remarkable recovery and Athens remained a major force in Greek politics. From the middle of the century Athens was locked in a struggle with the rising power of Macedon which culminated in the defeat of the Athenian and Theban armies at the battle of Chaironeia in 338. Athens was reduced to a Macedonian vassal. On the death of Alexander in 323, Athens joined the Greek revolt against Macedon. The revolt was suppressed and Athens was compelled to receive a Macedonian garrison and to impose a property qualification for citizenship, thus ending the full democracy. Democracy persisted in a more limited form, intermittently suppressed or further restricted, in the centuries after Alexander's death up to and after the subjugation of Greece by Rome; that story is beyond the scope of this book.

3

Democracy and Ideology

In this and the following chapters I deal with the functioning of the Athenian democracy. As far as possible I treat the classical period as a single entity, though where necessary divergences between the fifth and the fourth century are noted.

3.1 Democratic ideology

Although the democracy underwent changes, the principles on which the system was based remained the same. Classical sources agree in identifying freedom, *eleutheria*, and equality, *to ison*, as the key features of democracy:

> It is clear not just in one particular but in every way that equal right of speech (*isegorie*) is of enormous importance, since the Athenians under the tyranny were superior to none of their neighbours in war but when rid of the tyrants were far the best. This shows that when oppressed they were deliberately slack, since they were toiling for a master, but when they were set free each one of them was eager to achieve for himself.
>
> Herodotos 5.78

> So first of all they are free, and the city is full of freedom and free speech (*parrhesia*) and there is licence (*exousia*) within it for a man to do as he likes.
>
> Plato *Republic* 557B

> The basis of the democratic constitution is freedom (*eleutheria*) … One aspect of freedom is that all the citizens shall rule and be ruled in turn. For in fact justice under a democracy is equality according to number, not according to merit, and since this is the definition of

> justice, inevitably the mass is sovereign and whatever they decide must prevail and must count as justice ... So in a democracy the poor have more authority than the well-to-do, because they constitute a majority ... Another aspect is that a man lives as he pleases. For this, they say, is the purpose of freedom, since it is characteristic of a slave not to live as he pleases.
>
> Aristotle *Politics* 1317a40ff

> In the first place rule of the mass has the most noble title of all, equality before the law (*isonomia*) ... It holds offices by lot, it keeps those in office subject to audit, and opens all political planning to public discussion.
>
> Herodotos 3.80.6

> Firstly you started your speech with a false statement, stranger,
> in looking for a tyrant here. For the city is not ruled
> by one man but is free.
> And the people rules by alternating in turn
> each year. It does not give wealth
> the most but the poor man has an equal share (*ison*).
>
> 'Theseus' in Euripides' *Suppliant Women* 403–08

> It is agreed that there are three kinds of constitution in the whole world, dictatorship (*tyrannis*), oligarchy and democracy, and dictatorships and oligarchies are governed by the temperament of those in power, but democratic cities are governed by the established laws. You are aware, men of Athens, that in a democracy the persons of citizens and the constitution are protected by the laws, while dictators and oligarchs are protected by distrust and armed guards.
>
> Aischines 1.4–5

The most important feature of democratic freedom was the protection of the person. The Athenian citizen was protected by law from torture, and no citizen could be executed without trial. It is one of the recurrent criticisms of the Thirty that they killed large numbers of citizens without trial. Freedom also has a collective dimension. For Aristotle and Euripides' Theseus, it includes preventing the concentration of power in the hands of any one individual or group. This is achieved by restrictions on length of service (usually one year) and by restrictions on repeated tenure of office. No magistracy could be held twice,[1] with a few necessary exceptions. Not mentioned in our sources as a particular hallmark of democracy, but equally important for the distribution of power, is the use of boards of magistrates, which had the effect of diluting the power of any individual member. Again for Aristotle and Euripides' Theseus, freedom also includes the subordination of officials to control by the people.

A prominent feature of democratic freedom in our sources is the right of all citizens to live their lives as they see fit. The degree to which Athens in reality recognized individual freedom is hotly contested. The laws placed restrictions (for instance, in the areas of inheritance or sexual activity) and made demands on the individual (such as military service). But most of the restrictions on individual freedom related to the protection of polis or family or to activities which harmed others. Subject to compliance with the laws, the individual was protected against the arbitrary exercise of power by officials. It is in this sense that the individual is free to live as he chooses. It is difficult to draw comparisons with non-democratic constitutions, since we are poorly informed about specific Greek states. But it seems that the level of official intrusion in citizens' lives varied and that democracy was least prone to interfere.[2] If we may trust our sources, before the reforms of Ephialtes the Areiopagos acted not only as guardian of the laws but also guardian of morals and exercised a high degree of intrusion into what under the democracy were private activities.[3]

Included in the freedom of Athenian democracy was the right to behave in ways which advertised disaffection with the democratic system itself. Admiration for Sparta was widespread among wealthy Athenians, especially in the fifth century but even after Sparta had lost its aura of invincibility in the fourth century. For some it went as far as aping Spartan dress and manners, such as wearing the hair long, in contrast to the Athenian habit of cutting it short. Naturally, some suspicion attached to such people, especially during the Peloponnesian

War, and Aristophanes has his chorus of cavalrymen in *Knights* ask for indulgence for their dress on the ground of their military service to Athens.[4] Suspicion of such behaviour was at its height after the Thirty, who were loyally served by the cavalry, and the speaker of Lysias 16, under suspicion (probably correctly) of having served under the Thirty, urges his audience not to hold his appearance against him.[5] But no law ever forbade such flamboyant gestures of respect for Sparta.

The Athenians were equally tolerant of explicit criticism of the democracy. One dimension of 'live as one pleases' was freedom of speech, *parrhesia* (literally 'saying everything'). Euripidean tragedy includes debate on the strengths and weaknesses of democracy. Old Comedy both readily mocked leading political figures and also satirized contemporary political structures and processes such as the courts, so central to the democracy, and the administration of the empire. Sokrates was vocal in his objections to what he saw as the weaknesses of the system. Though in the end he paid with his life for his views in one of the less creditable acts of the restored democracy, it was his association with the members of the two oligarchic regimes rather than his criticism of democracy alone which prejudiced the outcome of his trial. His pupil Plato (ironically a champion of censorship) was perfectly free to publish his extensive criticisms of democracy, as in turn was Plato's pupil Aristotle.

The major exception to the tolerance of *parrhesia* was in the sphere of religion. In the late 330s a decree was passed on the initiative of Diopeithes allowing for prosecution for disbelief in the gods or the teaching of astronomy (with its substitution of material over theological explanations of the world).[6] The statement has been doubted, but there is no compelling reason to reject it. We have evidence for the (politically motivated) prosecution of a number of intellectuals for impiety in the final decades of the fifth century and of Sokrates, the most notorious example, at the beginning of the fourth. This restriction too (though obviously open to manipulation) falls into the category of the protection of the polis and reflects a need to remove possible causes of divine anger against the community at large. The prosecutions relate not to privately expressed beliefs but to public practice and teaching.

Equality consists in the right of access to the political process to all citizens without distinction of wealth or birth. This includes the right to hold office or to serve on a jury. Prominent among these rights is the one identified by our sources as *isegoria*, literally 'equal speech'. It was open to any citizen not only to attend but also to address the Assembly. Theseus in Euripides' *Suppliant Women* declares proudly:

> This is freedom: 'Who wishes to offer
> in public good advice he has for the city?'
>
> 438–9

It also includes equality of protection under and access to the law. Other constitutions could use the language of political equality, *isonomia*. The Thebans in Thucydides[7] use the term *oligarchia isonomos*, 'egalitarian oligarchy', without irony. What distinguishes democratic *isonomia* is not the concept of equality but the scale of its distribution within the polis.

Though it is useful for analytical purpose to distinguish the concepts of equality and freedom, the two are intertwined in discussions of democracy and are often barely distinguishable.

3.2 The limits of equality

But the ideology of equality had its limits. Equal access to political activity was never confused with an equal right or an equal ability to perform all tasks, though the opponents of democracy sometimes get confused on this issue. The Athenians, like all Greeks, believed that judgment comes with maturity, and at all times they discriminated on grounds of age. For service on a jury or the holding of office, the minimum age was 30.[8] There were other limitations on equality. Aristotle and others associate democracy with the use of selection by lot rather than election. But even under the democracy at its most radical some offices, specifically those requiring particular skills or experience, were always filled by election. It is worth noting the definition of equality given by Thucydides' Perikles:[9]

> It bears the name democracy because it is governed not by the few but by the majority. All have equal rights in law in private disputes; but when it comes to prestige, as each man is respected in some activity, he receives more honour in public affairs, not by rotation but on grounds of excellence, nor, with respect to poverty, if a man can do some good for the city, does he find himself prevented because of the obscurity of his station.

It is noteworthy that even here, in one of the most idealized presentations of Athenian democratic principles, there is no suggestion that all should expect to contribute to the city in the same way. The vision is of a meritocracy, in which individual authority is earned by personal ability, not acquired as an automatic right.

There is another respect in which the Athenians never sought equality. Plato's Sokrates makes the following claim at *Republic* 557a:

> Democracy, I think, comes about when the poor are victorious and kill some of the rich [literally 'the others'], exile others, and give the remainder of the population an equal share in political activity and office, and in general offices are filled in democracy by lot.

Democracy did in some cases arise from violent revolution. And attempts could be made, in ancient as in modern times, to sweep away the previous elite. But Plato's generalization is wildly inaccurate in the context of Athens, the only democracy he had encountered at close quarters. The fact that democracy in Athens came about through a series of evolutionary leaps rather than a single violent coup allowed it to retain and adapt aspects of the previous system. This capacity to evolve, adapt and absorb is an important part of the success and stability of Athenian democracy. In a much quoted statement, the *Athenian Constitution* reports the announcement made by the Eponymous Archon at the beginning of his term:[10]

> And the archon immediately on assuming office first of all announces that all the possessions a man had before the commencement of his service he is to keep and control until the end of his term.

It is generally supposed that this pronouncement goes back to the archaic period. It reflects the fear of a redistribution of land, a measure which some of the poor hoped for in Solon's day and which was a common demand in Greece at times of revolution. The ritual pronouncement was a constantly recurring reassurance that Athens was governed by law and that individual property, like the person, was protected under the law. There was no attempt to redistribute wealth from the rich to the poor, a common theme in some modern egalitarian ideologies. The Athenians accepted economic disparity as an inescapable fact of life. Though politically radical, Athenian democracy was economically and socially conservative.

Nor was there any attempt to bar the elite from power: instead, the democracy sought to harness traditional features of elite activity for the city as a whole. Since the time of Homer the rich and well-born had engaged in competition for prestige and influence, in war, in athletics and in politics. It was characteristic of the Greek polis regardless of constitution to appropriate this competition for its own purposes. The great achievement of Athens was to put elite competition to the service of mass democracy. The benefits for the city as a whole were considerable. The absorption of aristocratic competition into the democratic structures and processes provided an outlet for divisive drives which might otherwise have found expression in violent insurrection. It offered an incentive for the wealthy to identify their interests with those of the democratic state. But it also offered a clear statement of the subordination of the individual to the collective good. And it ensured that some at least of the conspicuous consumption of the rich was used for the benefit of the city as a whole.

The most obvious example of this process is in the political sphere, where the rich and influential compete for the favour of the demos. This favour was registered partly in tangible rewards but no less importantly in the intangible reward of prestige. Political activity offered the individual a means not only of achieving eminence for himself but also of bequeathing prestige to his family. Another area in which elite competition is put to the service of the democracy is the liturgy system, which is discussed in the next section.

The importance of elite competition for the democratic state is recognized by Demosthenes:[11]

> The equal share of privileges among those who have political power creates unanimity in oligarchic constitutions, but competition in which men of merit engage for the rewards granted by the people guarantees freedom in democracies.

In other words, the successful democracy divides and controls the elite. However, this is more than an issue of political calculation. The Athenians collectively – even under the democracy – retained a respect for wealth and birth. And although the Greeks inside and outside Athens recognized the danger that wealth could corrupt, they were also aware that poverty too could tempt people to crime.

3.3 Citizenship

As in other Greek states, the Athenians guarded the privilege of citizenship jealously. Any non-citizen who exercised citizen rights was liable to prosecution by an action called the *graphe xenias*, literally 'indictment for alienhood/foreignness', and if convicted the alien would be sold into slavery and his or her property seized and sold.

The qualifications for citizenship changed during the life of the democracy. Until 451/0 a man was eligible to exercise citizen rights, provided that his father was Athenian and his mother was of free birth, irrespective of her race. But in 451/0 Perikles carried a proposal to limit citizenship henceforth to those who could demonstrate Athenian birth on both sides.[12] Although the measure did not affect individuals who had qualified for citizenship under the previous definition from exercising their rights, it had the effect of nullifying marriages between citizens and foreigners and preventing such marriages for the future, since the resultant children would not quality for citizenship and would be classed as bastards for inheritance purposes and therefore unable to inherit more than a nominal sum from their father's estate.[13] The reasons for Perikles' measure are unclear. One obvious reason which suggests itself is a desire to restrict the economic benefits of democracy and empire; it can be no coincidence that the measure was passed in the decade which saw the introduction of pay for a range of political functions. But given the political importance and the self-confidence of Athens at this period, the measure may have been explicitly designed to convert the native Athenians into a closed and privileged group, a mass elite. By the middle of the fourth century, the law prescribed severe penalties (enslavement with confiscation of property) for foreigners who contracted or feigned a marriage with an Athenian citizen,[14] but it is not certain that these were part of the decree of 451/0.

The role of marriage in citizenship is a matter of continuing debate. The *Athenian Constitution* nowhere states explicitly that marriage was a precondition, and our other evidence is ambiguous. Modern scholars are divided on the issue. However, even if bastards were technically able to claim citizenship, it might have been difficult in practice to exercise the right, since there was no formal means for a father to acknowledge a bastard child. A father would normally admit his children to the *oikos*, the family unit, at a ceremony ten days after birth, but bastards were not full members of the *oikos*. Though the phratries, as sub-divisions of the old tribes, had lost formal political significance under the Kleisthenic reforms, membership of the phratry is often cited in court as evidence for parentage and indirectly for citizenship; but phratry membership was confined to legitimate male issue. In practice therefore it was difficult to prove parentage without proving legitimacy, so whatever the legal position may have been, there was a positive incentive for bastard sons of two Athenian parents to pass themselves off as legitimate.

The exercise of full citizen rights was confined to adult males. Women played no direct role in the public sphere in any area except religion. However, women had an integral part in the transmission of citizenship, as they did in the transmission of property, since (at least from 451/0) only a woman of full Athenian birth could give birth to citizens. Accordingly, the Athenians used the same terminology for males and females of full Athenian birth, *astos*/*aste* ('townsman', 'townswoman'), *polites*/*politis* ('man/woman of the polis').

Citizenship was based on deme membership, which was transmitted from father to son. An Athenian qualified for citizen rights on reaching the age of eighteen, though for the exercise of some rights there were additional age limits. To obtain citizenship, the Athenian was subjected to an examination (*dokimasia*) to test his qualifications. He was presented to his deme, who voted on whether he had reached the required age and whether he met the birth qualifications.[15] If the majority of the deme members were satisfied, his name was added to the deme register (*lexiarchikon grammateion*). Anyone rejected on grounds of age could reapply in subsequent years. Anyone rejected on grounds of birth could appeal to the courts. If the appeal succeeded, the deme was forced to enrol him; if it was unsuccessful, he was sold into slavery.

It was also possible for non-Athenians to be granted citizenship. But nowhere is the jealousy with which the Athenians guarded the privilege of citizenship more visible than in the area of naturalization. Citizenship was the top rung of an honours system (which included tax exemptions and the removal of some restrictions on the rights of foreigners) used to reward those outside the citizen body. It was bestowed comparatively rarely on outsiders. And it had to be earned by conspicuous service to the Athenian people. On occasion citizenship was awarded for service to the democracy, for instance to non-citizens who served in the fleet at the battle of Arginousai in 406[16] or the assassins of Phrynichos, one of the leaders of the oligarchs of 411. The inscription rewarding Phrynichos' killers survives.[17] Since opportunities for this kind of service were naturally few, in practice most citizenship awards were for economic benefactions, such as the donations in cash or military supplies of the wealthy banker Pasion[18] or for substantial assistance to the Athenian trade in various commodities but especially the grain supply (since Attica could not supply the needs of the population and Athens was heavily reliant on imported grain). Accordingly (with few exceptions) only rich aliens acquired Athenian citizenship. Awards of citizenship for service to Athenian trade included foreign rulers, for whom the award was purely honorific (since there was never any prospect of their exercising the rights). The loss of empire increased Athenian reliance on diplomatic gestures of this kind in the fourth century as a means to secure favourable arrangements for Athenian merchants.

The process for naturalization was designed to create obstacles. In most modern societies the acquisition of citizenship is an administrative matter. In Athens it was a legislative matter; citizenship could be granted only by a vote of the Assembly. Our fullest information concerns the procedure in the mid-fourth century. According to our source,[19] two meetings of the Assembly were required. At the first a citizen put forward a decree proposing citizenship. If there was a majority vote in favour, it had to be confirmed at a subsequent Assembly meeting; a quorum of 6,000 was required and the vote was taken by secret ballot to prevent intimidation or corruption. Even after this vote, the grant could be challenged, since the proposer could be prosecuted under the action available against illegal proposals (*graphe paranomon*), either on procedural grounds or because the individual honoured did not deserve the award, and if the prosecution succeeded the award was rescinded. Even once admitted to the citizenship, an alien was barred from serving as one of the nine archons or as priest.[20]

The term used for rights enjoyed by the Athenian citizen is *metechein tes politieias*, 'to have share in the constitution/political activity/citizenship', or *metechein tes poleos*, 'to have a share in the polis'. The rights are nowhere spelled out for us and it is doubtful that there was ever a formal legal list of them. Evidently there was a general consensus on what those rights were. The gulf between citizens and non-citizens in terms of rights was enormous and was daily re-enacted in a variety of ways. Most obviously, the citizens' rights include the right to attend and address the Assembly, to hold office or to serve on a jury. They also include the right to marry an Athenian woman and the right to own land in Attica. Non-Athenians could rent but could not own land or houses, though the right to acquire land (*ges enktesis*) could be granted to aliens as an honour. The citizen was also privileged in the legal system. Full access to the whole range of procedures allowed under the laws was reserved for the Athenian citizen; some procedures could not be brought by non-citizens.

Citizens were also privileged in having access to certain state benefits. People with a disability which prevented them from working could apply for a means-tested benefit (subject to an upper property limit of three mnai, three thousand drachmas); the dole was one obol per day early in the fourth century and two obols per day by the date of the composition of *Athenian Constitution*.[21] During the fourth century the state also handed out non-means-tested festival money (*theorika*, literally 'viewing/attendance money') to citizens; originally the aim seems to have been to allow attendance at the dramatic festivals, but it was also applied to a number of other festivals (effectively granting paid holiday). The state also, from the fifth century onward, undertook to pay for the maintenance of the children of Athenian citizens who were killed in battle,[22] a right which was extended to the children of those who died fighting against the Thirty, as we know from the fragments of Lysias' *Against Theozotides* and a partially preserved inscription.[23]

Finally, the citizen was privileged in religion. The rites of phratries were exclusive to citizens, and both at deme and at state level full participation across the range of festivals was a privilege reserved for the citizens. The relationship between status and religion is discussed further in Chapter 6.

In some modern societies citizens are legally obliged to vote. There was no formal obligation to become involved in the business of the city. The Athenian state relied heavily on individual initiative. It was for the volunteer (*ho boulomenos*) to address the Assembly. And, in the absence of a police force, for the most part it was up to the individual volunteer to take legal action against crimes affecting the state. But there was no legal obligation for the average citizen to do either.

The public duties of the citizen are often described in our sources as 'obeying orders' (*ta prostetagmena*/*ta prostattomena poiein*). These responsibilities lay predominantly in the military sphere. All Athenians were liable for military service. The kind of service depended on financial status. Those who could afford to buy and keep a horse served in the cavalry. Those who could afford heavy armour served as hoplites. The rest would serve either as light-armed troops (slingers, archers, javelin throwers), as rowers in the fleet, or as marines (*epibatai*), that is, heavily armed soldiers serving on-board ship, for which they were armed at state expense.[24] In the period after the Athenian defeat at Chaironeia in 338 there was a major innovation in military service with the reorganization of the *ephebeia*, 'cadetship' (from the Greek *hebe*, 'puberty'). The *ephebeia* was probably an old institution. But as part of a policy of ensuring preparedness for war, the institution was formalized. On reaching eighteen the Athenian youth of hoplite status was now required to spend two years in military training, including garrison duty.[25]

Liability for military service ended at the age of fifty-nine, when all citizens (or possibly all of hoplite status) could be required to act as public arbitrators for a year, as their last compulsory service for the state. In order to reduce the business of the courts, it was a requirement that most private lawsuits should go to public arbitration. The arbitrator's role was to effect a compromise, or failing that to give a judgment, which was subject to appeal to a court.[26] The role was not without its risks, since anyone who was convicted of misconduct as an arbitrator was subject to *atimia*, loss of citizen rights; this risk was real, as we see from the case of Straton in Demosthenes 21. 83–95.

For wealthier citizens, there were financial responsibilities in addition. Though there were numerous indirect taxes at Athens, classical Athens had no regular direct taxation except for resident aliens, who paid a monthly tax (the *metoikion*, 'metic tax'). There were intermittent property levies (*eisphorai*) imposed on the wealthy in times of war, but for the most part financial contributions from the rich were securely anchored to public service (*leitourgia*, 'liturgy'). Prominent among these was the *trierarchia*. The trierarch was given a warship and tackle by the state and was required to maintain it at sea for a year, though by the late fifth century, as the prolonged war with Sparta took its toll, we find trierachies divided between two individuals, and during the fourth century the burden became largely a financial contribution divided between boards of those liable. The other kind of liturgy was connected with public festivals. The most prominent among this category was the *choregia*. The *choregos* was given responsibility for a chorus either in the dramatic or the dithyrambic competitions (choral performances by men or boys) in the state festivals. This required him to pay their wages and cover costume and incidental costs. A partially preserved speech by Lysias (speech 21 in modern editions) suggests that in the early fourth century a tragic chorus might cost half a talent (3,000 drachmas), while a dithyrambic chorus (depending on the competition and the age of the chorus) might cost anything up to 5,000 drachmas (though this figure includes the tripod dedicated for the victory), at a time when the average daily wage for a labourer was probably about one drachma. The figure given there for service as trierarch (together with Lysias 19.42, 32.26) suggests that the full cost of a year's trierarchy might be in the region of fifty mnai (5,000 drachmas). Not all liturgies were as burdensome as the *choregia*. But it has been estimated that the total number of liturgies (excluding the *trierarchia*) was at least ninety-seven, rising to at least 118 every fourth year when the Great Panathenaia was celebrated (distinguished from the annual Panathenaia by additional pomp and athletic competitions intended to attract athletes and visitors from the whole of the Greek world).

Possession of citizen rights was for life; but it was conditional and the entitlement could be lost permanently or temporarily, in whole or in part. The term for loss of political rights was *atimia*, literally 'loss of honour/privilege'. Anyone subject to full *atimia* was barred from addressing the Council or the Assembly, holding office, serving on a jury or addressing a court in any capacity; he was also barred from the public temples and the Agora.[27] He could still marry within the citizen group (though his marriage prospects were poor); he retained his property and his right to own land, yet since he could not represent himself in law, he had to rely on friends and relatives to protect his person and property. In some respects a man in this position was worse off than a non-citizen, who could at least represent himself in court.

Figure 3.1 Panathenaic vase. Prizes in the Panathenaic games were multiples of vases of Attic olive oil.

Temporary *atimia* was the automatic result of any debt to the state. And if a man died owing money to the state, his sons inherited his *atimia* until the debt was paid in full. Permanent loss of citizen rights was imposed as a penalty for a number of offences which were felt to be incompatible with citizen status. These included failure to serve on a campaign when called up, desertion in battle, and throwing away one's shield, mistreatment of parents, or homosexual prostitution. The first of these reflects the dependence of the state on its citizen militia for its survival, even in the fourth century when the use of mercenary troops was widespread. The severity of the treatment of those guilty of abuse of parents is based in part on the emphasis placed on respect for parents in Greek belief in general and in part on the interest of the state in the protection of the family. The penalty for homosexual prostitution is at first sight surprising in a culture where there was a widespread (though not universal) recognition of homosexual activity as natural. The law is explained by Aischines on the grounds that a man who had sold his body would sell anything, and was therefore singularly corruptible.[28] The claim could be true. Certainly it has to have a degree of plausibility to appeal to his audience. But the context is the prosecution of a political opponent for having prostituted himself in his youth and may reflect Aischines' rhetorical needs as much as any consensus. The root of the Athenian attitude may lie in the male military ethos; a man who sold himself had assumed a passive role more compatible with female than with male stereotypes.

4

The Core Bodies

4.1 The Council

Technically the Council of 500 (*Boule*) is an *arche*, a board of magistrates, and in principle is no different from the countless small boards which administered Athens; this is reflected in the rules for appointment, and vetting before and audit after tenure of office. However, the scale of the central role played by the Council in the democratic administration and its close relationship with the Assembly justify its inclusion here. Its importance is reflected in the fact that it heads the account of the magistracies in the description in the *Athenian Constitution*[1] of the constitution prevailing in the late fourth century. It is also shown in the readiness of prominent politicians to serve in the Council at critical periods, such as Kleon in the mid-420s and Demosthenes in 347/6,[2] during the run-up to the Peace of Philokrates between Athens and Philip of Macedon.

Council members were selected by lot, fifty from each tribe.[3] As with other magistracies, the minimum age for membership was thirty. The selection was based on the demes, the numbers from each deme depending on its size. In addition a further 500 substitutes (*epilachontes*) were selected by lot. Like all public officials, members of the Council were subject to a preliminary scrutiny (*dokimasia*) to test their formal eligibility, and the substitute would take office in place of any member who was rejected. On passing their scrutiny they took an oath, whose most important clauses were that they would serve according to the laws and in the best interests of city and demos.[4] By the late fourth century, members were paid five obols for each day of attendance.[5] There is some evidence that men of property were disproportionately represented in the Council membership, and the rate of pay (below that for a labourer at this period) suggests the same. The Council was excepted from the general rule barring reselection for the same office; it was possible to serve twice in the Council. The exception reflects the potential difficulty of finding 500 fresh citizens over thirty every year willing to serve, though in fact it is relatively rare to find people serving twice.

The Council met daily, except for annual festivals.[6] Meetings were open to the public, who were separated from the members by a fence, though it could meet in secret, if circumstances required.[7] Voting at its meeting was by show of hands, except when it was acting in a judicial capacity, when secret ballot (the norm in Athenian trials) was used.

A body of 500 is fairly cumbersome, and so the Council of 500 had an executive committee to handle business between Council meetings. This executive committee was formed by giving the representatives of each tribe responsibility in rotation for one tenth of the year. The title given to the tribal group was Prytaneis and the period of office was called *prytaneia*, anglicized as 'prytany'. The ten *prytaneiai* formed the basis of the administrative year, which functioned alongside the lunar calendar of twelve months which operated for religious and most practical purposes. During their period of office the Prytaneis dined at state expense at a building in the Agora called the Tholos; they had an allowance of one obol per day for food.[8]

A chairman of the Prytaneis was selected by lot.[9] As with almost all offices in Athens, this could be held only once. It lasted for a day and a night, during which he held the city's seal and the keys to the temples and the public records. He had to remain on duty during that period, accompanied by a third of the Prytaneis. They slept in the Tholos, so that there was always a contingent of the Council on duty in case urgent action was needed. That this was more than just a theoretical possibility can be seen from Demosthenes' account of one such emergency (though in this case the incident happened while all the Prytaneis were still present), when the news arrived in 339 that Philip of Macedon had seized Elateia in Phokis and was within an easy march of Attica:[10]

> It was evening, and someone brought the news to the Prytaneis that Elateia had been taken. At this they immediately rose in the middle of their dinner. Some of them drove the shopkeepers out of their booths in the Agora and burned the wicker frames, while others sent for the generals and called a trumpeter. And the city was full of confusion.

The Council as a whole acted as the steering committee for the Assembly. It gave prior consideration to Assembly business and set the agenda for the Assembly meetings. The Council placed business before the Assembly in the form of a *probouleuma*, 'preliminary motion'. These could carry a recommendation from the Council proposing a specific decision (often termed by modern scholars a 'closed *probouleuma*'), which the Assembly was free to accept, reject or amend in the light of debate and alternative proposals put forward at the Assembly meeting, or they might be open-ended, simply proposing discussion of an issue without making a firm recommendation (often termed an 'open *probouleuma*'). Only items which had been discussed by the Council could be put to the Assembly vote[11] and a proposal could be challenged by *graphe paranomon* if it was *aprobouleutos*, not covered by a preliminary vote from the Council. In its role as steering committee, the Council received envoys from foreign states and granted them leave to address the Assembly.[12] Athenian envoys to other states reported to the Council on their return.[13]

The Council also acted in many respects as the executive arm of the Assembly. The Council published its own decrees (these begin: *edoxe tei boulei*, 'the Council resolved'), which generally deal with routine matters or with specific decisions devolved to it by the Assembly. In carrying out specific activities on the instructions of the Assembly it was no different from any other board of magistrates. It was its routine functions (some of which were carried out by subcommittees) which made it the Assembly's representative. The *Athenian Constitution* sums up the Council's role with the words: 'it also co-operates in most of the activities of the other magistracies.'[14]

Foremost among these functions was finance. The multiple sources of income and the large number of officials handling public money meant that direct supervision by the Assembly was never a realistic possibility. This supervision was devolved to the Council.

The Athenian state possessed substantial amounts of property and revenue-generating activities. The Athenians preferred not to run these activities directly in the manner of modern state-owned industries and bureaucracies, but instead put them out to contract. The silver mines under the soil, even under private land, were the property of the state. The right to work these mines for a specified period was auctioned by officials called the 'Sellers' (*poletai*). It was the Council that voted on the bids.[15] A similar process applied to the right to collect the 2 per cent tax on imports and exports, the right to collect the monthly metic tax (*metoikion*), and the right to collect the state tax on prostitutes (male and female); these concessions were farmed out by auction to the highest bidder.[16] The profit for the successful bidder was the difference between the amount paid to the state and the tax collected. The sacred land attached to public shrines was leased out by the King-Archon, the *Basileus*, in the presence of the Council.[17] The Council also supervised the sale of private property confiscated by the state from people convicted of intentional homicide and political crimes.[18]

The Council also had overall responsibility for the receipt of money due to the state. The successful bidders for leases and taxes paid either in a lump sum in the ninth prytany or in instalments. The Council, together with officials known as the 'Receivers', *apodektai*, took receipt of these payments.[19] In the fifth century, it was the Council which received the tribute from the cities of the empire.[20]

The financial role of the Council included general supervision of the expenditure of officials. During the fifth century payments from the public treasury were made as needed by the Kolakretai, who were supervised by the Council; this role disappeared in the fourth century, when the various boards received their own budgets under an annual distribution (*merismos*). The Council appointed officials (*logistai*, 'auditors') who examined the accounts of magistrates every prytany and the officials who vetted the accounts of the magistrates at the end of their period of office.[21] Oversight of expenditure included supervision

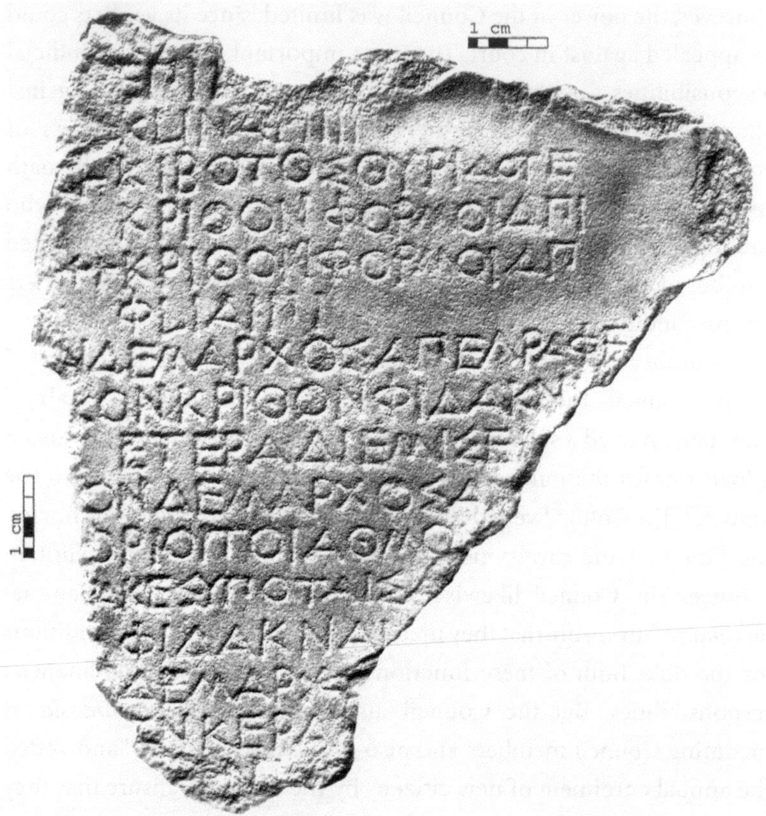

Figure 4.1 Inscription recording the sale of confiscated property.

of the placing of contracts for public works. By the 320s this task had been passed to the courts but it seems that the Council continued to supervise projects in progress and maintenance work.[22]

The Council also had military responsibilities, primarily in connection with the navy. They were obliged to ensure that a specified number of ships were constructed each year.[23]

The Council had a judicial role, and the *Athenian Constitution* credits it with judicial authority over other magistrates.[24] This kind of oversight was exercised by the Areiopagos before the reforms of Ephialtes.

However, the power of the Council was limited, since its verdicts could be appealed against in court. The most important aspect of its judicial responsibilities was the receipt of impeachments (*eisangeliai*) against offcials for offences against the state. The Council had powers of arrest, most notably in cases of suspected treason,[25] though the oath sworn by its members precluded the imprisonment of a citizen who could provide appropriate guarantees against flight, except in a limited number of cases. It also had the power to eject any of its own members for misconduct.[26]

A number of formal examinations (*dokimasiai*) were also conducted by the Council. These included an annual *dokimasia* of the cavalry.[27] The state invested a substantial amount in the cavalry, since it advanced a loan toward the purchase of the horse and also contributed to the fodder.[28] The Council vetted the fitness and the treatment of the horses, the fitness of the cavalrymen and their financial ability to maintain a horse. The Council likewise subjected the disabled to an annual *dokimasia*[29] to ensure that they met the physical and financial conditions for the dole. Both of these functions are connected with its financial responsibilities. But the Council also conducted the *dokimasia* of incoming Council members and also of the nine archons[30] and vetted the annual enrolment of new citizens by the demes to ensure that they were old enough.[31]

4.2 The Assembly

Modern democracy is almost always representative democracy. Except for referenda, more common in some systems than in others, the population as a whole exercises political control indirectly through individuals or parties which it elects at intervals to perform executive and legislative functions for a fixed term. Athens, in contrast, was a direct democracy. Power was exercised by the people regularly, at short intervals, and on specific issues. Athens had no government in the modern sense as a clearly defined entity distinguishable from the population as a whole. The demos of adult male citizens was the government, and its term of office had no time limit.

The two means by which the people of Athens exercised control were the Assembly and the lawcourts. The Assembly (*ekklesia*) was the sovereign body of the state with continuing responsibility for state policy. Though the demos never met as a whole (Athens never had a meeting place which could accommodate them all), the Assembly was conceptualized as the citizen population in session. Athenian authors generally use the term 'the demos' to refer to the Assembly, and inscriptions recording decrees of the Assembly refer to 'the demos', not 'the Assembly meeting' (*ekklesia*): they begin: *edoxe toi demoi*, 'the demos resolved' or *edoxe tei boulei kai toi demoi*, 'the Council and the demos resolved' (where the Assembly ratified a Council recommendation). Foremost among the responsibilities of the Assembly were issues of peace, war and alliance, the elections of officials whose positions called for expertise which precluded the use of the lot, and the continuing oversight of public officials.

In the fifth century it was also the legislative body and laws that could be passed by a majority vote in the Assembly, provided that the matter was placed on the agenda by the Council.[32] From the time of the restoration in 403 we find a different procedure in place, however. The chronology and relationship of the various laws on the subject are not entirely clear,[33] and the issue is complicated further by the nature of the sources available; some of the information comes from documents preserved in the medieval texts of lawcourt speeches which may be fabrications from the Hellenistic period. But the consistent (and irrefutable) element is the selection of 'legislators', *nomothetai*, from among those who had been empanelled for the year as jurors in the courts. The Assembly still retained overall control, in that proposals for new laws or the repeal of existing laws came before the Assembly for discussion in the first instance. It was the Assembly which decided whether *nomothetai* were needed.

In the fourth century the Assembly was required by law to meet four times each prytany. In the fifth century, the laws were less prescriptive.

We hear of one occasion in 431 when Perikles avoided having an Assembly meeting for forty days,[34] from which it has been inferred that the minimum prescription at that time was one meeting each prytany.

Although any citizen could address the Assembly, this does not mean that any issue could be raised at will. The agenda for discussion was set by the Council.[35] During the fourth century at least there were specific fixed items of business which dominated part of the agenda. The arrangements in place for the 320s are described at *Athenian Constitution* 43.4–6. The first meeting of each prytany was called the Principal Assembly, *kyria ekklesia*. At this meeting the Assembly voted on the conduct of officials. Two other major issues figured on this agenda: grain supply and defence. Political impeachments (*eisangeliai*) could also be made at these meetings. The likelihood of large attendance attracted by the nature of the business at these meetings explains the other regular items on the agenda. Confiscations of property (which would in due course be auctioned) by the state were announced. So too were claims on inheritances and for the hand of heiresses (*epikleroi*), that is females whose father had died leaving no male heir (in such cases Athenian law allowed the nearest male relative to claim her). In the sixth prytany there were additional items on the agenda of the Principal Assembly: a vote was taken whether to hold an ostracism (even in the fourth century, long after ostracism had been abandoned in practice). It was possible also to bring accusations against individuals alleged to have abused the judicial system to bring false accusations in order to persecute, blackmail or extract dishonest profit (the term for such an individual was *sykophantes*) and against anyone who had made a false promise to the demos. At the second meeting in each prytany any individual could make formal supplication to appeal for the support of the demos on any public or personal matter. Aischines mentions one such incident: in 348 a number of Athenians were among the captives when Philip of Macedon took Olynthus in the north and their relatives appealed to the Assembly for assistance.[36] The other twenty Assembly meetings per year had no prescribed business beyond the requirement that each must have three items relating to religious matters, three on secular matters, and three dealing with embassies. These were minimum, not maximum numbers; so the rules did not prevent such issues from coming up as often as circumstances demanded.

In addition to the regular meetings, there was scope for extraordinary meetings (*ekklesiai synkletoi*, 'summoned Assemblies') to deal with business which could not wait for the normal cycle. For most of our period the Assembly also acted as a court under the procedure of *eisangelia* ('impeachment') as well as receiving accusations. Under the *eisangelia* procedure an accusation was lodged before the Council or the Assembly. The Council's jurisdiction in *eisangelia* extended only to offences committed by officials; the Assembly in contrast could receive accusations against anyone for crimes against the state. Since the Council only had limited punitive powers, even in those cases which did fall within its jurisdiction any serious allegation coming before it would be passed to the courts. For the fifth and the first half of the fourth century the Assembly itself tried *eisangeliai* made before it; these hearings required additional Assembly meetings. But from the middle of the fourth century the *eisangelia* hearings were transferred to the courts.

In the absence of hard figures, it is difficult to determine how many Athenians attended Assembly meetings. The scale of the auditorium on the Pnyx hill where the Assembly met is of little use as a guide, since this cannot be plotted with confidence over the classical period. During the fifth century the capacity was about 6,000. It has been suggested that the auditorium was increased in size when the Pnyx was reshaped at the end of the century, which would attest at least the expectation of higher attendance figures. But the issue is contentious and the answer depends on a subjective judgment on the location of the speaker's platform in this phase.

A more useful place to start is the quorum for special votes. For all votes dealing with an individual, whether ostracism in the fifth century or (in the fourth century at least) grants of citizenship, there was a quorum of 6,000. This means that an attendance of 6,000 citizens was always a realistic possibility, especially since in the fourth century (when grants of citizenship were more frequent than in the fifth) there must have been several such meetings a year. But the absence of the 6,000 quorum for ordinary meetings indicates that attendance on this scale could not be guaranteed. On the basis of the quorum of 6,000 for certain meetings, we can conjecture a minimum regular attendance of about 4,500 at a very conservative estimate and more probably at least 5,000. On this basis the attendance for meetings with a quorum would increase by 20 per cent to 33 per cent. This is in itself a dramatic increase. Even if we accept that the importance of the subject generated a heightened interest, any lower estimate for ordinary meetings must assume an unrealistic increase for special votes. On any calculation, the Athenians were an unusually politicized population. It is impossible to determine a firm figure for the citizen population in the absence of any census during the lifetime of the democracy. The citizen population (that is, the adult male Athenians) varied with the effects of plague (in the late fifth century) and war but is estimated to have been between 20,000 and 30,000 at various times. That up to 6,000 citizens, perhaps 20–25 per cent of the total, could be expected to attend the Assembly, even for special votes, is remarkable.

However, the *Athenian Constitution* suggests that there were problems with attendance and that this was the reason for the introduction of pay for attendance at the Assembly at the beginning of the fourth century. It would be unwise to take this as evidence for poor attendance in the fifth century. The Peloponnesian War generated significant fluctuations in attendance due to military service,[37] but the absence of any known attempt to introduce pay in the fifth century suggests that there was no great anxiety about numbers. We also know that the oligarchic conspirators of 411 had to resort to a trick to create an audience sympathetic to their constitutional proposals. They held the Assembly meeting outside the city walls, in order to deter attendance by those without heavy armour, who would be especially vulnerable in the event of an attack by the Spartan army based at that time at Dekeleia.[38] The need for the trick suggests that a large mass attendance could be expected at a normal Assembly meeting. The introduction of pay may reflect special factors at work immediately after the restoration. The population had been depleted by war, and in particular the deaths of men of military age will have skewed the population to some degree toward the elderly, who would be less mobile and (in the case of those who lived outside the city) less likely to undertake the walk to Athens. Economic hardship arising from the war will have discouraged people from taking time off for politics. But the date of the introduction of pay (shortly after the restoration, at a period marked by a desire to stabilize and protect the constitution) suggests that the brief statement about poor attendance in the *Athenian Constitution* oversimplifies. It is likely that the concern was not simply to maintain absolute numbers but to ensure that the Assembly contained a cross-section of the population and that poorer citizens were represented, a matter of inevitable concern after two oligarchic revolutions in a decade. The means of implementation (universal rather than targeted pay) resembles the theoric fund and may reflect a desire to avoid both the administrative complexity and the odium of means-tested payments. But the increase in the rate of pay during the fourth century (while jury pay remained static at three obols per session) suggests that the concern about Assembly attendance persisted. The rate was set by Agyrrios immediately after the restoration at one obol per meeting, a nominal sum; it was raised by Herakleides to two obols, a sum then outbid by Agyrrios, who raised it to three obols, half a drachma; all this happened within the first decade of the fourth century.[39] Although this looks in part like a competition for popular favour, it also seems to indicate that attendance remained, or continued to be perceived as, a problem; and by the time of the composition of the *Athenian Constitution* in the 320s the rate of pay was a drachma for an ordinary meeting and nine obols for a Principal Assembly, depending on the nature of the meeting.[40]

It is difficult to be precise about the composition of the Assembly meetings. Hints in speeches made to the Assembly are an unreliable guide, given the small number which survive and the likelihood that these reflect the rhetorical needs of the speaker as much as the make-up of the historical audience. Modern experience of meetings in any context suggests that attendance will have varied. The arrangements for the Assembly agenda presuppose this, since ten meetings a year were intended to deal with core issues of crucial importance for popular control or essential for the wellbeing of the state. We can guess with confidence that there was a hard core of fairly regular attenders among those in the city or in the adjacent countryside. For those in and around the city attendance was probably easier for people engaged in agriculture, with its irregular demands on time, than for groups such as small shopkeepers and craftsmen reliant on regular trade, though even these would be able to attend, if they had a slave or family member who could take over as needed. Attendance from the more distant parts of Attica will have been both limited and patchy. Even for those living within, say, twenty-five kilometres of the city attendance will have involved an overnight stay, and anyone living a few kilometres away would still have had a pre-dawn walk of at least an hour. But even so, with only forty meetings a year, regular attendance was a possibility for those who were seriously committed to participation. The attractions of visits to the city for buying, selling, curiosity and visits to relatives must have offered those outside Athens an incentive for at least intermittent attendance. It has been suggested that monied citizens were a significant presence in the Assembly. There is no way of testing this proposition. But we can be reasonably sure that they were never an effective force for reaction, for the Assembly consistently, both in the fifth and fourth centuries, increased the popular control over the various aspects of the political process.

During the fifth century the *prytaneis*, the standing committee of the Council, presided over Assembly meetings. For much if not all of the fourth century meetings both of the Council and of the Assembly were chaired by a body of nine *proedroi* selected on the day of the meeting from within the Council,[41] one from each tribal contingent except the one serving as *prytaneis*. The presiding officials were assisted in maintaining order by the Scythian archers, the slave corps who performed a (very) limited range of police functions in Athens.[42]

We can reconstruct the procedures for meetings of the Assembly both from accounts of real meetings and from Aristophanes, who several times (in *Acharnians, Women at the Thesmophoria* and *Assemblywomen*) offers parodies of the procedures. Meetings began early; in *Assemblywomen* the women, who have disguised themselves as men in order to push through a measure to transfer control of the state to women, make their way to the Pnyx at dawn, as does the hero of *Acharnians*.[43] In the 420s at least there were measures in place to ensure prompt arrival. The Pnyx was adjacent to the Agora, which as the main shopping area as well as the administrative centre of the city offered a wealth of inducements to loiter. From *Acharnians* 21–2 it seems that a rope smeared with red dye was drawn through the Agora in order to herd people toward the Pnyx and to mark latecomers. During the fourth century, the introduction of pay for attendance at the Assembly made it easier to ensure good timekeeping, since from *Assemblywomen* 391–80 it appears that at least at that period only a fixed number qualified for pay.

The meetings began with a purificatory sacrifice. A pig was slaughtered and its blood sprinkled round the periphery of the Pnyx. Pollution played an important part in Greek belief and the purification ensured that the participants were not contaminated or deliberations put at risk by the presence of anyone who was ritually unclean. The herald then uttered a prayer and a curse,[44] which unfortunately is best known from a parody in Aristophanes' *Women at the Thesmophoria*, but which was evidently directed against any speaker who took bribes, deceived the demos or threatened the constitution or the city. Before the Assembly convened, the *prytaneis* made a sacrifice and (as was usual with animal sacrifice in the ancient world) the sacrifice itself was interpreted as an omen and the results reported to the Assembly.[45]

The proceedings proper began with an invitation from the herald: *Tis agoreuein bouletai,* 'Who wishes to speak?' According to Aischines, originally the invitation ran: 'Who wishes to speak of those who are above the age of fifty?' Once the older men had spoken, the rest were invited to speak.[46] But this practice had certainly died out by the middle of the fourth century, and possibly much earlier.

Assembly meetings could be very lively. Thucydides' account of the Assembly at which Kleon received the Pylos command in 425 gives some idea of just how lively:[47]

> And [Kleon] with indirect reference to Nikias, who was serving as general and whose enemy he was, and taunting him, said that if the generals were men, they would set sail and capture the men on the island, and this is what he would have done if he were in command. And Nikias, because the Athenian were yelling to Kleon for not setting sail right now, if he thought it easy, and because he could see that Kleon was taunting him, urged him to take whatever force he saw fit and attempt it, as far as they were concerned. Kleon initially was willing, while he thought that Nikias was pretending to offer to give up command, but when he realized that Nikias was keen to give way to him, he retreated and declared that not he but Nikias was general ... And they did what one would expect of the mob; the more Kleon sought to evade the voyage and retreat from what he had said, the more they urged on Nikias to hand over the command and shouted to Kleon to sail.

According to Thucydides, Kleon's bluff was called by the Assembly. Given the speed with which Kleon took control of the military situation, his plans for the campaign (based on the military experience of the general Demosthenes) were presumably already laid and he may have been manipulating the Assembly (though given his inexperience of military command some nervousness would be natural). But there is no reason to doubt the broad account of the meeting, which was evidently boisterous. Plato presents this as a consistent and unhealthy quality of the Assembly:[48]

> 'Why, when,' I said, 'a large crowd are seated together in assemblies or in court-rooms or theatres or camps or any other mass public gathering, and with loud uproar express disapproval of some of the things that are said and done and approve others, both in excess, with loud clamour and clapping of hands, and beyond this the rocks and the

> region round about re-echoing redouble the din of the criticism and the praise.'

Plato, like his teacher Sokrates, was no fan of Athenian democracy and we should not put too much trust in this picture. Although Plato presents the Assembly as raucous and undisciplined, surviving decrees show that the Assembly could generate sustained and detailed debate and that it was possible for the clerks to follow the proceedings. Not infrequently we find decrees consisting of several segments, in which a substantive motion is followed by subsidiary proposals which expand or refine the main motion. A good example is the decree honouring the assassins of Phrynichos:[49]

> In the archonship of Glaukippos, when Lobon of Kedoi was secretary. The Council and the demos resolved, when the tribe Hippothontis was serving as *prytaneis*, Lobon was secretary, Philistides was presiding, and Glaukippos was archon. Erasinides proposed: That Thrasyboulos [of Kalydon] be praised because he is a good man toward the Athenian demos and eager to do it whatever good he can ... Diokles proposed: That all else be as proposed by the Council, and Thrasyboulos should be an Athenian and should enrol himself in any tribe and phratry he wishes ... Eudikos proposed: That all else be as proposed by Diokles. But on the issue of the people who took bribes relating to the decree you passed for Apollodoros ...

This is not chaos.

The herald asked: 'Who wishes to speak?' We cannot hope to know how often ordinary citizens answered this call and stood up to address the demos. We have evidence for proposals in the Assembly from people who are otherwise unknown. Some, possibly most, of this can be (and has been) explained away; some may be members of the Council simply performing a routine function by presenting a preliminary motion (*probouleuma*) already approved by the Council. Some may be acting as front-men for more high-profile figures or for factions. But the emphasis in our sources on *isegoria* suggests that interventions from people who spoke rarely, or only once, must have been a real possibility. We have to distinguish these from the regular speakers, who were always few in number. And they were almost always from the upper end of the economic scale. The ordinary Athenians controlled the debate, but not by active participation on the speaker's platform; they did so collectively, by heckling and with their vote, and subsequently by punishing speakers for failure.[50]

After the debate, the presiding officials would put proposals to the vote. Except for ostracism votes in the fifth century and votes on naturalization, voting in the Assembly was by show of hands (*cheirotonia*, literally 'hand-stretching'). This included both the election of officials and votes to depose officials. We have no evidence for precise counts of votes, which can be confusing in modern parliamentary systems with smaller numbers, and would be especially difficult even in a poorly attended meeting, and it is generally supposed that a rough count sufficed.

4.3 The Courts

The other important organ of popular political control was the lawcourts (*dikasteria*), manned by 6,000 jurors (*dikastai*). Commenting on the constitution operating in the 320s, the *Athenian Constitution* observes:[51] "The demos has made itself master of everything, and it governs everything through decrees and lawcourts, in which the demos has the power.' The political importance of the courts is recognized in the account of Solon, where his introduction of the right of appeal to a court is seen as one of the most democratic of Solon's measures:[52] 'when the people have control of the vote, they gain control of the political system'; the language used (*psephos*, secret ballot) means that 'vote' here is the one cast in court, not the open vote by show of hands in the Assembly (*cheirotonia*). The intimate connection between courts and Assembly under the democracy is acknowledged by speakers addressing the courts, who frequently say 'you decided' or 'you enacted' when referring to executive decisions by the Assembly or legislation, as though the two were identical. How far the two groups, Assemblygoers and jurors, really overlapped in composition is impossible to determine with any degree of confidence. As in the case of the Assembly, scholars have attempted to extract information on the social background of the jurors from the assumptions apparently underlying statements in surviving speeches, but again the evidence is unreliable. I discuss the composition of the jury panels further below. What we can say is that the Athenians were confident that the Assembly and juries shared the same ideology, as can be seen from the progressive increase in the involvement of the courts in the political process during the fourth century.

Though the jurors did not sit as a single body but were divided into panels numbering hundreds or even thousands, depending on the kind of case, they are treated by contemporary writers as though they were a single organ. Speakers addressing the court tend to ascribe decisions by any other court to the jury in front of them, as in the following example:[53]

> I am informed, jurors, that a certain Bakchios, who was condemned to death in your court, and Aristokrates, the man with bad eyes, and others of that sort including Konon here were comrades as young men and had the name 'Triballians' [the name of a wild Thracian tribe].

Jury service was confined to citizens over the age of thirty. The 6,000 were enrolled for a year at a time and were selected by lot from all who applied. Once selected, they swore an oath (of which the most important clauses were to listen to both sides without fear or favour and to judge according to the laws). Though it has been estimated that the courts may have sat between 175 and 225 days a year, the number of courts needed on any one day, and therefore the likelihood of being selected for service, varied. When pay for jury service was introduced in the fifth century, the rate was set at two obols a day. The pay was raised to three obols by Kleon in the 420s.[54] Though inflation drove up general rates of pay in the fourth century, including pay for attendance at Assembly meetings, the rate for jury service remained the same. So we can be sure that there was no difficulty in getting people to serve. We are badly informed about the composition of the jury panels, though. Jurors were not obliged to turn up every day and for many of them jury service may have been seasonal employment or a fallback when other work was not available. This would have appealed, for instance, to farmers or people in the building trade. Shop-owners and craftsmen who had family members or slaves who could carry on their work in their absence might also have welcomed the opportunity to supplement the family income with jury service. Aristophanes in *Wasps* represents the juries as composed primarily of old men. Though he probably exaggerates, regular attendance must have been of interest to people (including the aged and the infirm) who found it difficult to obtain more strenuous or more lucrative work. The *Athenian Constitution* (though reflecting a biased source) suggests that jury service did not attract wealthier members of society.[55] But otherwise there was probably a mix of age, background and interest groups. From *Wasps*, it seems that in the fifth century jurors were allocated to a single court for the year.[56] This system was open to corruption, and in fact there is evidence for some jury tampering late in the fifth century.[57] Early in the fourth century elaborate procedures were put in place to make the allocation of jurors to courts unpredictable and these were further refined by the 320s.[58]

Service on the judicial panels was not an office (*arche*); so there was no limit on length of service and no audit (*euthynai*). The jurors were, like the Assemblygoers, answerable to nobody. This idea is exploited mercilessly in Aristophanes' satirical presentation of the jurors in *Wasps* in 423 as irresponsible and vindictive old men with delusions of grandeur. We should take this with a generous pinch of salt. Speakers addressing the juries universally expect the jurors to care about issues of fact, law and justice and devote a great deal of space to convincing them on these grounds. But the power of the jurors collectively was considerable. The jury panels served as both judge and jury; though each court had an official presiding, his role was to control proceedings, not to advise on matters of law or direct the jurors. And as representatives of the Athenian demos, their decisions were not subject to appeal.

There was in Athens no police force or state prosecution service. Some officials were charged with enforcing the law in their area but their role and powers were circumscribed. In court as elsewhere the initiative in almost all cases lay with the ordinary citizen. The chief division in Athenian law was between public and private cases. Private cases were held to be a matter between the individuals concerned and so only the alleged victim could take action. Public cases were held to concern the state as a whole and prosecution was open to anyone (the Athenians used the term *ho boulomenos*, 'the volunteer'); these cases included both offences against the polis and acts which had an individual victim but were viewed as impacting more generally on society or where the victim for one reason or another was not in a position to take legal action.

The courts were used to try cases of alleged political misconduct, such as receipt of bribes or treason. Accusations of this sort played an important role in the process of competition between politicians, who tended to impute malice and criminality to their opponents rather than error. But the courts were not confined to high crimes; they were also formally embedded in the normal political process. Proposals in the Assembly could be challenged by the procedure of *graphe paranomon* (indictment for illegality). Under this procedure any citizen could prosecute the proposer on the grounds that the proposal was procedurally flawed or that its substance contravened existing legislation. If the measure had not yet been passed, further consideration was suspended while the case was heard; even after the measure had been passed, the proposer remained open to prosecution by *graphe paranomon* for a year. In the event of conviction the measure fell and the proposer was liable to a punishment assessed by the court. Three convictions brought loss of political rights. The earliest trial under this procedure known to us took place in 415.[59] Though we cannot rule out the possibility that the *graphe paranomon* was introduced earlier, perhaps under the reforms of Ephialtes, the absence of evidence for earlier cases suggests that it postdates the 420s. In the fifth century *graphe paranomon* could be invoked against both laws and decrees.

But the firm distinction between laws and decrees after the restoration brought a need for an additional measure. From now on *graphe paranomon* was invoked against decrees, while *graphe nomon me epitedeion theinai* ('indictment for passing a disadvantageous law') was available against proposers of new laws.

The preliminary vetting of public officials (*dokimasia*) also involved the courts, which would hear appeals from those rejected. In the case of the archons there was an automatic double *dokimasia*, first before the Council and then before a court.[60] The courts also heard appeals from youths rejected by their deme at their *dokimasia* when they applied for admission on reaching the age of eighteen. At the end of his term of office each official was subject to an examination (*euthynai*) of his conduct. This consisted of two stages, the first devoted to their financial accounts, the second to their general conduct; at the latter stage it was open to anyone to lodge a complaint.[61] Allegations of financial or other misconduct would be tried by the courts.

During the fourth century the use of members of jury panels was extended to include a key role in the legislative process. The *nomothetai* responsible for the vetting of new legislation and amendments to existing legislation were drawn from the 6,000 who had sworn the jurors' oath.[62]

It would be a mistake, however, to imagine that the political role of the courts was confined to these explicit functions. Above and beyond the overtly and unambiguously political use of the courts, we find politicians using ostensibly non-political cases to harry their rivals. The opportunities for attack were increased by the possibility of using agents to prosecute political enemies, or of appearing as witnesses or supporting speakers in court. And politicians could also be attacked indirectly. For instance, we have evidence for the prosecution of intellectuals associated with Perikles for impiety;[63] this looks like an attempt to taint Perikles by association and undermine his popularity. One of the most diverting of the courtroom speeches which survive is the speech *Against Neaira* ([Demosthenes]59), which was delivered for the prosecution of an ageing prostitute, Neaira. The real target was her lover, the minor politician Stephanos, and again the aim was to taint by association.

Through the succession of political cases coming before them, the courts acted as an additional forum for testing the popularity of politicians and policies as well as deciding on the specific issues which formed the basis of the trials. Since the courts could reverse decisions of the Assembly, through the operation of *graphe paranomon*, and (in the fourth century) through the *graphe nomon me epitedeion theinai*, it could be (and has been) maintained that the courts were the supreme authority in the state; and in fact this claim is sometimes made by speakers addressing the courts. But such statements should be treated with caution. Though speakers might treat them as a single body, the jury panels collectively lacked cohesion and unlike the Assembly had no power of initiative; their role was reactive only and they did not constitute a distinct power base.

5

Serving the Democracy

5.1 The servants of the demos

In comparison with any modern democracy, the Athenian system was very simple. The structure of the administration meant that there was no need for a substantial central bureaucracy. The contracting out of activities such as taxation removed the need for a specialized revenue service. The use of the volunteer system for prosecutions meant that there was no need for an extensive network of legal administrators. And there was no police force. The law regulated some aspects of the operation of schools, but otherwise the state was not involved in formal education; schools were private. The polis appointed and paid a retaining fee to a number of doctors[1] but beyond this there was no health service to maintain and there were no hospitals.

But by ancient Greek standards the Athenian state was a highly complicated organization, and for some fifth-century observers the radical democracy was marked by an excess of bureaucracy.[2] The Assembly could decree, but for the implementation of its decisions it required administrators. To run the daily business of democracy, a small army of officials was required. These effectively acted as the civil service of Athens. However, the parallel is inexact. Civil servants in most modern democracies are, along with the judiciary, the source of continuity. Politicians come and go. And in some systems the most senior public servants come and go with the politicians. But there is always a large number of low- to middle-ranking, and in some systems senior, civil servants who form the bedrock of the political operation and ensure a continuity of expertise and a transfer of knowledge. It was precisely this concentration of experience that the Athenian system of annual rotation and the rule preventing repetition of service in the same office was designed to avoid.

The number of public officials was much greater in the fifth century than in the fourth, since the empire generated an enormous amount of administrative business. The *Athenian Constitution* gives a figure of 700 Athenian domestic officials and 700 overseas officials for the middle of the fifth century.[3] The repetition of the same figure suggests that the text has been corrupted in transmission. Unfortunately it is impossible to tell which figure is wrong and by how much. The various internal officials listed for the fourth century in *Athenian Constitution* add up to over 300, excluding the Council; and the list is incomplete. Modern research suggests that a figure in advance of 500 is entirely possible, so 700 may not be a wild exaggeration. The *Athenian Constitution* subdivides these officials into those selected by lot and those elected by show of hands in the Assembly.

5.2 Officials selected by lot

In Athens the vast majority of public offices were filled by random selection from among those who put themselves forward. The use of lot is regarded by our ancient sources as characteristic of democracy. The lot is the absolute leveller, placing rich and poor on the same footing and removing opportunities to influence the outcome, either through canvassing or through corruption. What is most striking about the use of the lot in Athens is the sheer range of areas where it applied.

We find officials with a supervisory capacity comparable, for instance, with those in modern departments of trading standards, weights and measures, customs and excise. These include the ten *agoranomoi*, 'market officers', who ensured that the goods on sale were unadulterated and genuine, the ten *metronomoi*, 'measures officers', who tested weights and measures, the twenty (originally ten) *sitophylakes*, 'grain inspectors', who prevented overpricing of grain and excessive mark-up on bread and flour, the ten *emporiou epimeletai*, 'trading zone supervisors', whose duties included ensuring that two-thirds of the grain which came into the port was transferred to the city.[4]

We find officials who carry out the function of sanitary and planning officers: the ten *astynomoi*, 'town officers', had the task of ensuring that maintenance work on private buildings did not cause nuisance or obstruction.[5] Their duties included controlling the price of entertainers at symposia and competition for their services, presumably to prevent public order problems from drunken customers. They also had control over the dung collectors who cleared the streets (apart from horse, donkey and dog excrement, such as one would expect to find in the streets, the Greeks were in the habit of using alleyways as latrines, and the same word, *laura*, serves for both) and they had responsibility for collecting the bodies of any who died in the streets. Among the officials responsible for public works we find the five *hodopoioi*, 'commissioners for roads', who controlled a team of slave labourers who maintained the roads.[6]

We also find officials with responsibilities for specific areas of the justice system, such as the five *eisagogeis*, 'introducers', who had the job of admitting and chairing a wide range of legal cases, the Forty, who had responsibility for most private cases, and the Eleven, who had charge of prisoners and executions.[7]

Another category is financial officers, such as the ten *poletai*, 'sellers', who auctioned leases, concessions and confiscated property;[8] a number of inscriptional records of the *poletai* survive, including the sale of the property of those implicated in the mutilation of the Herms in 415.[9] This category also includes the ten *apodektai*, 'receivers', who received money paid to the state and (in the fourth century) paid it out to the various boards of officials in proportion to their share of the *merismos*, and the ten *logistai*, 'auditors' and their assistants who vetted the accounts of officials at the end of their term of office.[10] Finally, some religious officials were appointed by lot, such as the two boards of *hieropoioi*, 'commissioners for sacrifices', ten of each;[11] one of these boards dealt with sacrifices ordered by oracles, the other primarily with most of the sacrifices at festivals which recurred at four-yearly intervals.

One body of officials selected by lot deserves separate treatment, the nine Archons. These consisted of six Thesmothetai, plus the King-Archon (in Greek simply *ho basileus*, 'the king'), the Polemarchos and the Eponymous Archon (in Greek simply *ho archon*, 'the archon') who gave his name to the year; in addition there was a secretary to the board. Even in the late fourth century the nine Archons were paid only four obols per day each, from which they had to pay for a herald and a flute-player to attend them.[12] The pay cannot have covered the expenses, and so the archonship retained a degree of social exclusivity.

The work of the six Thesmothetai was predominantly legal. They had responsibility for a range of cases distinguished either by their importance or the need for speed.[13] This included receiving the complaints, handling the preliminary hearings and chairing the resultant trials. The three archons each had their own individual tasks. The Eponymous Archon had responsibility for a number of festivals, including selecting the playwrights to compete at the Dionysia and assigning each a chorus-producer (*choregos*). He received appeals from individuals selected for the role of chorus-producer. He presided over a number of legal cases, many involving the family, for which he had a special responsibility. The King-Archon's duties were primarily religious. These included overall responsibility for the Eleusinian Mysteries. The cases over which he presided also had a religious dimension, including, and especially, homicide trials. The Polemarchos had been, until the early fifth century, the chief military officer of the state. This role was still reflected under the democracy in his religious duties, which included the games held in honour of the war dead. The principal legal role of the Polemarchos was in relation to cases involving metics, again reflecting his early role as the leader in state contact with aliens.[14]

The duties of the three oldest archonships were demanding, especially since they exercised most of them as individuals, not as members of a board. It was presumably for this reason that each of them was allowed to appoint two assistants.[15] Some of the individuals identified as assistants to the Archons were (or became) active politicians and this system allowed the Archons to draw on additional expertise.

Most of the offices filled by lot involved routine activities; the system of boards reduced the burden of responsibility on each individual, meaning that people of modest means and ambitions could undertake them. Hence we find Demosthenes distinguishing between the rich man undertaking elective tasks such as the role of envoy and 'a poor man, an ordinary citizen with little experience who has served in an allotted office'.[16] The contrast is forced, like all contrasts in the orators; and of course 'rich' and 'poor' are elastic terms. But probably Demosthenes is right to see the division between election by show of hands and the lot as mirroring both a social divide and a distinction in terms of political experience and ambition. But even the administrative tasks filled by lot were not mechanical. All carried responsibility, though usually shared and exercised within firm guidelines. To the modern age of entrenched bureaucracies the use of lot on this scale, combined with the loss of expertise caused by the obligatory annual turnover of personnel, seems a hopelessly inefficient way to get state jobs done. But the whole point of this system is diametrically opposite to the modern management-orientated notion of leaving public business to experts and functionaries. It seeks to disperse power and political experience as widely as possible among the population, not to concentrate it among a small coterie. Efficiency is not its primary goal.

It is more difficult to judge the effectiveness of the system. The lot was an aspect of the democratic constitution which attracted criticism. Sokrates is represented in our ancient sources as critical of the use of the lot for the selection of officials.[17] Presumably like most administrative systems, the lot produced its fair share of administrative incompetence. But so do modern systems in which administrators are appointed and promoted on the basis of experience. And the use of boards meant that the damage done by any one individual was likely to be small. The procedures for examining the conduct of officials on completion of their term of office would act as some deterrent to the dishonest and inept, and there were mechanisms to depose corrupt or incompetent officials. The fact that the use of lot was gradually extended during the life of the democracy, combined with the readiness of the Athenians to use election where the work merited it, indicates that, whatever its ancient critics might say, the Athenians found that on the whole the system worked in practice.

5.3 Elected officials

Although the lot was crucial to democratic ideology, the Athenians themselves were aware that it had its limitations. Lot can be used for duties which require qualities which are reasonably common (such as common sense, judgment, integrity, efficiency). It is less useful for jobs requiring specific skills and experience. And the more important the decisions taken, the more risky the reliance on lot. Posts requiring a high degree of expertise were filled by election by show of hands (*cheirotonia*) in the Assembly. Likewise, because of the need for continuity the usual restrictions on reselection did not apply in the case of these posts. Here we are moving into the world of (what we would call) the professional.

The posts emphasized in *Athenian Constitution* as belonging to this category are the most obvious ones, the military offices.[18] This applied to all of them. At the top were the ten generals (*strategoi*). In the fifth century they functioned as a board but during the fourth century they were each given specific responsibilities. Each tribal infantry contingent was commanded by a taxiarch (*taxiarchos*) and each tribal cavalry contingent by a phylarch (*phylarchos*, 'tribal commander'). In addition, there were two hipparchs (*hipparchoi*, 'commanders of horse') with overall command of the cavalry, subordinate to the generals.

Given the crucial importance of the water supply in the dry climate of Greece, it is not surprising that the *epimeletes ton krenon*, 'supervisor of the springs', was elected.[19]

The other major area where election plays a significant role is finance. Though routine financial management was left to the relevant boards under the supervision of the Council, there were some posts where the scale of the income or expenditure or the importance of the policy decisions involved placed them beyond routine competence. In the fifth century the officials responsible for the accounts of the Athenian empire, the *Hellenotamiai* ('treasurers of the Greeks'), were probably elected (a possible but not inevitable inference from the presence of politically prominent figures among their number). During the fourth century we find individual financial officials and boards in operation in areas where traditionally the Council would have had oversight. The treasurer of the military fund, *tamias ton stratiotikon*, was elected.[20] During the period of military expansion following the creation of the Second Athenian League in 378, this fund received the unspent residue which the administrative boards received under the *merismos*. In the 350s, with the emergence of a more cautious foreign policy in the wake of the Social War, which cost Athens the more important members of the League, the annual budgetary surpluses were transferred into the theoric fund, and the fund was used not only to provide for citizen attendance at festivals but also for major public works, both defensive and civil.[21] The officials in charge (*hoi epi to theorikon*) were elected.[22] The importance of this board can be seen from the fact that leading political figures were eager to serve on it: Euboulos in the 350s, Demosthenes and Demades in the 330s. By the 320s the treasurer of the military fund and the officials in charge of the theoric fund collaborated with the Council in the allocation of mine leases and contracts for tax-collection.[23] From the mid-330s the politican Lykourgos controlled Athenian finance for a period of twelve years.[24] The details of his position remain obscure but his post may have been *ho epi tei dioikesei*, 'official for the administration'.[25]

5.4 The secretariat

The officials we have been considering required clerical support. Unfortunately, we are badly informed about the minor functionaries who serviced the boards. The more significant secretarial posts were filled by lot or election, exactly like the boards themselves. For instance, the Council had a 'prytany secretary' (*grammateus kata prytaneian*), who attended Council meetings and took minutes and kept the records. He was originally elected but by the 320s was selected by lot. The Council 'law secretary' (*grammateus epi tous nomous*), who wrote down the texts of legislation coming before the Council, was selected by lot, as was the secretary of the Thesmothetai. The secretary who read out the documents to the Council and the Assembly (there were no agenda papers and no drafts of proposals were circulated) was elected.[26] These secretaries might in turn have under-secretaries (Greek *hypogrammateus*) working for them. The less significant posts were filled by professionals or by slaves. It was at this lower level that the continuity needed for effective running of a state with a high administrative turnover was maintained. For instance, the secretary who assisted the Receivers and kept the records of payments due was a public slave, as was the clerk who looked after the public records in the records office in the Agora.[27] Various other minor roles were filled by slaves, such as the public executioner.[28] In order to limit the influence of the professional secretaries, by the early fourth century it was forbidden for anyone to serve twice as under-secretary to the same board.[29] However, this would not prevent a secretary circulating among the boards and we find at least one case (Nikomachos, attacked in Lysias 30) of a secretary working his way up to a position of some importance in the redrafting of the laws before and after the restoration.

The secretary would often be the point of contact for anyone doing business with the boards of officials.[30] Not surprisingly, as is often the case with minor bureaucrats, there appears to have been a popular prejudice against such people. Aristophanes in *Frogs* has Aischylos complain that the city is overrun with under-secretaries, and Demosthenes is able to exploit his opponent Aischines' early career as an under-secretary against him.[31]

5.5 Public speakers

Various terms are used by the Athenians to designate active politicians. The verb *politeuesthai* means simply 'be a citizen', but those who conspicuously use their right to participate in the city's affairs are described as a class as *hoi politeuomenoi* 'those who are active in politics'. The term *demagogos*, 'leader of the demos', is also used, sometimes (from critics of democracy) with a perceptible air of disapproval (like the modern derivative 'demagogue'), though equally it can have a neutral sense. More common in the latter part of the fifth century is the term *prostates tou demou*, 'champion/protector of the *demos*'. From the late fifth century the term *rhetor*, 'speaker', becomes common as a generic term for politicians. Its frequency reflects the fact that public speech before the Assembly was the way to shape policy under the democracy.

For much of the fifth century the post of general was held by major political figures. People like Perikles owed their credibility with the people in part to their military successes. But during the last third of the century we find a divorce between military and political leadership, with the Assembly dominated by speakers who owe their authority to their oratorical skills and political judgment, not to their military proficiency, though even after Perikles we find figures like Nikias and Alkibiades combining activity in the Assembly with military command. During the fourth century there is an almost complete separation between military command and public speaking.[32] Though we still occasionally find people who combine regular intervention in debate with military command, notably Phokion from the middle of the century, the more common pattern was for public speakers to forge alliances with generals. The combination of major elective posts with activity on the Pnyx re-emerges from the middle of the fourth century. The difference is that it was now financial, not military, office which was sought. However, in the age of Demosthenes, as in the age of Perikles, the Pnyx was the centre of political power. A brief exchange in Aristophanes' *Peace* neatly sums up the realities of democratic politics. The goddess Peace, newly rescued by the hero Trygaios from the cave in which she had been imprisoned, asks (through the god Hermes) for news of Athens:[33]

Hermes: And now hear what next she just asked me:
who now has control of the stone [i.e. the rostrum] on the Pnyx?
Trygaios: Hyperbolos is now master of that terrain.

We occasionally find individuals who influence politics from behind the scenes, like Antiphon in the fifth century, of whom Thucydides observes: 'he preferred not to appear in the Assembly or in any other public meeting, but though he was distrusted by the mass because of his reputation for cleverness, he was nonetheless more able than anyone else to aid anyone on trial in the courts or in the Assembly who consulted him.'[34] But it is no coincidence that Antiphon was the leading light in the oligarchic coup of 411.

To the modern reader of Thucydides or Xenophon, perhaps the most striking aspect of political debate is the emphasis placed on the individual. This is especially true of the stylized debates in Thucydides, where the competing views are set against each other in the form of matching speeches, creating a verbal contest which is reminiscent of the duel of the Homeric hero. In the absence of political parties (a relatively recent development in democratic systems), it was up to the individual to convince the demos that his policy was the right one. And his popularity was tested repeatedly in successive Assembly meetings. But this does not mean that there were no political alliances. We have evidence for groupings of politicians who shared the same view on specific issues, generally clustered round a single dominant figure. Aristophanes gives a vivid portrayal of such a group in his description of his bugbear Kleon (cast in the role of a mythical monster):[35]

> From his eyes flashed the most fearsome rays of Kynne [a courtesan],
> while a hundred heads of cursed flatterers licked
> about his head, and he had the voice of a death-dealing torrent.

The 'flatterers' here are the lesser members of Kleon's political group. But these associations lacked the cohesion of modern political parties. They were essentially personal alliances; though some were long-lasting, at certain times – particularly in the middle of the fourth century when Athens had to face the rising power of Macedon – we find kaleidoscopic shifts of allegiance. Unlike many modern democracies, where the serious competition is between two political parties, at Athens there were usually several groups operating at any one time. For instance, in the middle of the fourth century we can plausibly identify at least three groups in action, the supporters of peace with Macedon as necessary for Athens' long-term security, the hardliners who opposed any accommodation with Macedon, and those who favoured peace as a temporary measure. At the beginning of the century as many as six factions have been identified.

Despite his central role in Athenian politics, the public speaker was never a public official. There is some evidence that limited attempts were made to formalize the role of the public speaker. Though we have no precise evidence for the date of the laws in question, the use of the word *rhetor* as a semi-technical term for a regular speaker in the Assembly points to the late fifth century at the earliest, and the most plausible period is at or after the restoration of 403. One source claims that the law required *rhetores* to have children and land in Attica, that is, they should have stake in the country they saw fit to advise.[36] This would place them on a par with generals and phylarchs.[37] However, even if our source is reliable, there is no evidence that the law was applied strictly in practice. More certain is the procedure called *dokimasia rhetoron*, 'scrutiny of public speakers'. Despite its name, this was a kind of legal action. It could be activated by any citizen and involved an accusation that a *rhetor* was barred from addressing the Assembly. Our only surviving example is the case brought by Aischines against Timarchos in 346, based on an accusation that he had prostituted himself as a young man (Aischines 1). Other grounds we know of were mistreatment of parents, military offences and squandering one's inheritance. The penalty imposed if the jury found for the prosecution was loss of citizen rights. The use of the term *dokimasia* assimilates the *rhetor* to state officials. But there is a crucial difference: unlike other *dokimasia* procedures, this was not automatic but had to be initiated by a volunteer prosecutor (*ho boulomenos)*. The role of the *rhetor* was never fully formalized.

There is a very good reason for this. Though the Athenians were aware that the regular speakers in the Assembly made up a minute proportion of the citizen population, it would have undermined the democratic principle of free speech to professionalize this activity. In this respect, modern translations of the term *rhetor* as 'politician', though often inevitable, blur a vital difference. The public speaker was a professional only in the limited sense that he devoted a major proportion of his time to politics. He received no salary from the state. As a result, we rarely find a regular speaker who comes from a genuinely underprivileged background. To dedicate one's time to political activity in such a system requires leisure, and therefore money, either from land or from manufacture and trade. Even the institution of pay for attendance at the Assembly made little difference to this system. An active politician needed free time between Assembly meetings to plan and to negotiate with potential allies. Diodotos, Kleon's opponent in Thucydides' account of the Mytilenaean debate of 427, observes:[38]

> In matters of the greatest importance and on an issue of this nature, we must look further ahead when we speak than you who give matters brief consideration, especially as we are responsible for when we give advice while you bear no responsibility when you listen to us.

The role of litigation in politics meant further that an active politician also needed sufficient time to be in court as prosecutor, defendant, witness or supporting speaker, as well as funds to meet fines if successfully prosecuted by opponents. Money was also needed to pay agents to prosecute one's political enemies. Though not essential, lavish performance of liturgies was an invaluable way for the aspiring politician to demonstrate his patriotism. In the fifth century, and even occasionally in the fourth century, this practice was extended beyond the festivals of the polis. We find men with political ambitions using victories in the great panhellenic athletic festivals (then as now a source of collective pride) as a basis for public prominence and popularity, an aristocratic practice as old as the ill-advised Kylon, who was an Olympic victor.[39] In Thucydides' account of the debate preceding the Sicilian expedition, Alkibiades exploits his success in the Olympic chariot-race as a claim to popular respect.[40] All this meant that the Athenian who had to work his land or hire out his labour had little prospect of penetrating the circle of influence. With rare exceptions, anyone wishing to play a continuing role in the Assembly needed to have considerable private wealth from large-scale farming or from trade or manufacture.

Since the *rhetor* had no formal position, there could be no formal apprenticeship. The aspiring politician would attach himself to one of the existing political groupings and make himself useful in a variety of ways. The speech *Against Neaira* describes the early career of a minor politician of the mid-fourth century, Stephanos:[41]

> Stephanos here had no income worth mentioning from political activity; he was not yet a public speaker but still only a sykophant, the sort who shout by the speaker's platform and hire themselves to bring indictments and denunciations and put their names to other people's proposals, until he fell under the influence of Kallistratos of Aphidna.

The speaker is attacking an enemy, so the route to influence is presented in the worst possible light. But the picture of the minor politician as a member of a claque in the Assembly (intended to exaggerate the support for a given speaker and so influence the voting), as a front man for proposals in the Assembly, and as a prosecutor used against political opponents of a faction or its leader, is both plausible and consistent with what we learn from other sources. Especially noteworthy here is the reference to prosecutions. In Athens, as in republican Rome, one way for the aspiring politician to achieve notoriety was to prosecute prominent figures. Perikles early in his career prosecuted Kimon, the leading politician of the 460s; Hyperbolos began his career in a similar vein.[42]

As in most political systems, very few politicians made it to the top, which in Athens meant being the leading member of a political group.

5.6 Accountability, risk and reward

Under the democracy, supreme power rested with the demos. This power is registered vividly in the dramatic metaphor of Aristophanes'

Knights, where Demos personified is presented as a householder, with the politicians as his slaves. An important aspect of the exercise of this power was the accountability of public officials. Either directly through the Assembly or the courts, or indirectly through the Council, the demos exercised a close scrutiny over its servants. Through the procedures for *dokimasia* on commencement of office, *euthynai* on termination of office, the regular opportunities each prytany for deposition of officials, or through the opportunities for political charges through the courts, the demos was able to maintain its control. This control was increased by the fragmentation of administrative power through the use of boards rather than individuals, since, unless all were corrupted together, members of each board could be expected to watch each other.

The punishment for misconduct could be severe. Antiphon, warning the jurors against a hasty decision, reminds them of an occasion when the whole board of the Hellenotamiai were condemned to death:[43]

> Again, your Hellenotamiai, when accused falsely, as I am now, of theft, were put to death out of anger rather than reason, all but one; and the truth was discovered subsequently. This one man – they say his name was Sosias – had been condemned to death but had not yet been executed. Meanwhile it was revealed how the money was lost and the man was set free by your assembly, though he had already been handed over to the Eleven; but the others had all been killed, though they were completely innocent.

Greek orators lied with ease, but a dramatic invention like this could not be sneaked past an audience, and so probably he is telling the truth, though he may be embroidering details.

But the risks were unevenly distributed. It was the elected officials who were especially exposed, the generals above all. Operating at long range, they were required to show initiative. But inevitably in so doing they risked incurring the anger of the demos if plans backfired. The demos had high, sometimes unrealistic, expectations of their military commanders and the price for disappointing those expectations could be severe. Perikles was deposed as general in 430, tried and fined, when the lack of success in the Peloponnesian War against Sparta was compounded by the suffering caused by the plague which afflicted Athens at the beginning of the war.[44] The generals who returned to Athens from an expedition to Sicily in 424, having failed to bring off the military success the Athenians expected – the Sicilians had temporarily put aside their differences to deprive Athens of an opportunity to intervene – were tried for corruption and severely punished; two were exiled and one was fined.[45] The generals who failed to pick up the wounded after the naval battle of Arginousai in 406 were tried all together and those foolish enough to return were executed.[46] Though the collective trial was unconstitutional, there is no reason to doubt that the generals would have been severely punished if they had been given a proper trial. We have evidence for a large number of trials of generals during the fourth century, resulting in enormous fines or executions. Timotheus, for instance, who played a major role in the creation of the Second Athenian League, was tried for treason in 356/5 and fined 100 talents.[47]

Envoys to other Greek states were also in an exposed position. These too might be called upon to make decisions on their own initiative, for which they might find themselves under attack on their return. The Athenian envoys who went to Macedon in 346 to receive Philip's oath under the Peace of Philokrates found the capital full of envoys from other Greek states. The Third Sacred War was still in progress between the Phokians who had seized Delphi in 356 and a number of states, in particular Thebes. Philip was preparing a campaign to settle the war and all the envoys were trying to secure a settlement favourable to their own state. Aischines wanted the Athenian group to intervene. According to Aischines, Demosthenes was more cautious:[48]

> Philip is setting off to Thermopylai; I cover my eyes. Nobody is going to put me on trial for Philip's military exploits but for any statement I make that I should not or any action beyond my instructions.

Aischines may misrepresent Demosthenes. But an envoy might well feel vulnerable. Aischines was charged with corruption for his role in negotiating the peace with Macedon. He was acquitted when he came to trial in 343. But another envoy, Philokrates, the main proponent of the peace, felt that its unpopularity made his conviction a certainty; he fled when impeached by Hypereides and was tried and condemned in his absence. The Athenian envoys who in 392/1 at a conference agreed to peace terms which the Assembly rejected were likewise tried and condemned in absence.[49]

The severity with which generals and envoys were treated reflects in part the difficulty of democratic control at such distances and the consequent need for deterrence through exemplary punishments. We have excellent anecdotal evidence that the deterrent force was felt by those for whom it was intended in Diodoros' account in the behaviour of the general Chabrias at the battle of Naxos in 376. Chabrias broke off his pursuit of the residue of the defeated Spartan fleet to rescue the Athenian wounded, because he remembered the lesson of Arginousai.[50]

Though the public speakers were not technically officials, they too were answerable for the advice they gave the Assembly. The risks for public speakers, either from explicitly political trials or from trials where the political agenda lurked behind an ostensibly non-political charge, were considerable. They rarely faced death; as a rule a public speaker who was condemned to death was convicted in another capacity (such as envoy or general), perhaps because it was often difficult to attach a particular setback unambiguously to a single speaker. But enormous fines were common, often on a scale designed to impoverish even a rich man and eradicate him as a political force, or to leave him a debtor to the state and therefore deprived of political rights. Politics is always a tough business. But the readiness of politicians bringing prosecutions to demand severe penalties strikes the modern as vindictive. However, this treatment of politics as a process of outright winners and outright losers with little between (a 'zero-sum game') was almost inevitable within the political structures in operation. In a direct democracy with no formal political parties, there was no procedure to give a political group an extended mandate to pursue its policies. A politician could influence policy indefinitely and only extreme measures could be guaranteed to neutralize him. Not all trials of course were calculated to break a career. Adverse verdicts and hefty fines (or acquittal) served to adjust the relative standing of individuals and groups and to complement the Assembly in determining the direction of public policy.

For much of the fifth century, political leaders were subject to the ostracism vote. Unlike political trials, the ostracism vote did not require an allegation of misconduct, merely a commitment from the demos to hold a vote, a quorum of 6,000, and enough anxiety or ill-will toward an individual to ensure him the largest share of the votes. The name, Greek *ostrakismos*, 'potsherd vote', is derived from the scraps of pottery (*ostraka*) on which the names of the targets were scratched. Plutarch tells a story about an encounter of Aristeides with an illiterate Athenian who without recognizing him asked him to write 'Aristeides' on the shard 'because I'm tired of hearing him everywhere called "the just"'.[51] Though suspect like all such anecdotes, the story accurately reflects the absence of the need for any substantive charge. There was a rash of ostracisms in the 480s, but they subsquently became less frequent. Victims included Themistokles, ostracized in the late 470s, possibly as the result of a struggle between pro- and anti-Spartan elements in Athens. Another was Kimon, ostracized in the late 460s; Kimon had staked his credibility on a policy of firm friendship with Sparta and his expulsion was probably concerted with the reforms of Ephialtes as part of a simultaneous restructuring of internal politics and external realignment with democratic Argos. Thucydides the son of Melesias was ostracized in the late 440s, thus leaving Perikles as the dominant figure in Athenian politics. Whatever its origin, in practice the principle driving the use of ostracism seems to be the need for a firm choice either between individuals or between policies. Though there was a free (any name could be inscribed) and secret vote, political factions worked hard to influence the result. The substantial numbers of shards showing the same name written in a single hand probably indicate not only the existence of a minor service industry in writing names for the illiterate but also the production by political factions of ready-made votes for distribution to those attending. One of the names on these pre-inscribed shards is Hyperbolos, the victim of the last ostracism, and the evidence of the shards agrees with Plutarch's account of the manoeuvring by the factions of Nikias and Alkibiades against him.[52] The ostracism fell into disuse after this. Though it remained available for use and as late as the 320s the vote was still taken whether to hold an ostracism,[53] it seems to have had symbolic value only at this point. According to Plutarch the procedure was abandoned because its use for a contemptible figure like Hyperbolos brought it into disrepute. Plutarch's account draws heavily on the comic depiction of Hyperbolos and on Thucydides' evident contempt for him.[54] So we should not take it too seriously. In fact, ostracism was a blunt instrument; it removed discord but at considerable cost by depriving the city of a potentially useful individual for ten years. With the availability of more subtle means of control, in particular the *graphe paranomon*, the ostracism may simply have seemed rather crude.

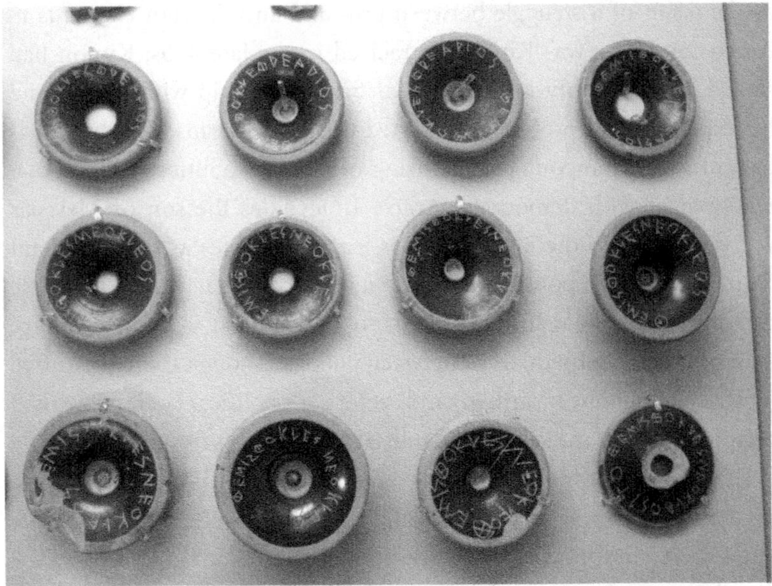

Figure 5.1 *Ostraka* inscribed with the name of Themistokles.

Public speakers were also subject to the law governing the procedure of *eisangelia* ('impeachment'), one clause of which classed the taking of bribes by a speaker to misguide the Assembly as treason.[55] However, the most common weapon against public speakers was the indictment for illegal proposals, *graphe paranomon*.[56] *Graphe paranomon* played a central role in Athenian political rivalries. According to Aischines, the politician Aristophon boasted that he had been unsuccessfully prosecuted by *graphe paranomon* 75 times.[57] Aischines may be exaggerating, and the length of Aristophon's career (he was active in politics for over half a century) probably made him unusual. But still the figure shows that prosecution by *graphe paranomon* was an occupational hazard for politicians. Though the public speaker was not technically an officer of the state, the activity was not risk-free.

Given the risks, it may seem surprising that so many members of the elite were eager to compete for the favour of the demos. But if the risks were great, so were the rewards. Indeed, the material rewards were considerable. Though public speakers were not paid, our ancient sources agree in seeing politics as a path to wealth. Old Comedy is full of allegations of corruption against politicians as a class and the politicians themselves freely hurled accusations of taking bribes at each other. Probably politicians did receive large sums in 'gifts' from states and individuals, either for specific favours or merely to secure goodwill. Such practices in one form or another are common in modern political systems, ranging from help with electoral and other expenses through to consultancies, directorships and various favours in kind bestowed on politicians by business and other interests. As we have seen, taking bribes to speak against the city's interests was an offence. This meant that there was always the risk of attack. But the fact that the law on *eisangelia* explicitly limits itself to cases where a speaker accepts money and 'does not give the best advice to the demos'[58] suggests that Hypereides is giving us a view which many Athenians could recognize when he says:[59]

> You readily allow the generals and the public speakers to receive considerable rewards. They have received this right not from the laws

> but from your leniency and generosity. You impose just one condition, that the money they receive should be through their influence with you, not against your interests.

The problem is that what constitutes taking money against the interests of Athens is open to subjective and hostile interpretation.

But it would be a mistake to focus solely on financial benefits. The Greeks, including the Athenians, were highly sensitive to issues of honour and dishonour. The successful politician amassed enormous prestige. This could be measured in formal awards (more common in the fourth than in the fifth century) such as crowns, gilded or otherwise, preserved on stone inscriptions which would serve as a permanent record. But this prestige was publicly recognized in less tangible but no less important ways through continuing influence in the Assembly and (as supporting speaker or witness) in the courts. And in a society which always viewed the individual within the family context, this prestige continued to be enjoyed by future generations, as we can see in the tendency of speakers in court to claim credit for the achievements of ancestors.

6

Religion in the Democratic City

As will be clear from the preceding chapters, we cannot understand democratic Athens, or any other Greek society, solely in secular terms. Religion was embedded in the daily life of individual and society to a degree matched by few cultures in the modern world. There was no group, whether formal or informal, which was not also in some sense a religious entity, from the family up to the state and beyond to Greece itself. Family, deme, genos, phratry, army and polis all had a ritual dimension as well as a practical role. Religious myths, beliefs, acts and sites all played an important role in shaping and sustaining individual and collective sense of identity.

The central importance of religion to the state can be seen from the statement in *Athenian Constitution* 43.6 that matters of religion formed a fixed (and opening) item on the agenda at the second and third meetings of the Assembly each prytany.[1] The degree of religious control by the polis can also be seen from the fact that to gain official status, any new cult had to be approved by the Assembly. This symbiosis between the secular and the sacred extends to financial dealings. Greek temples received dedications; the more important the temple the bigger, the richer and more plentiful the dedications. Land owned by temples was usually leased out, providing a further source of income. Their wealth and their relationship with communities at different levels gave temples an additional and invaluable role as banks. At the beginning of the Peloponnesian War the Athenians deposited 1,000 talents with the temple of Athene on the Acropolis (the Parthenon) to draw down as needed.[2] But as well as serving as a safe deposit box, this and other temples offered loans to the demos at favourable rates.

At a more basic level, all collective activity involved some element of religious ritual. As we saw, meetings of the Assembly were enveloped in

Figure 6.1 Parthenon.

religious acts (see p. 169). As well as securing divine favour, these rituals also served to impress upon all present the significance of the occasion and a sense of their own status and role. At meetings of the Boule, the members prayed to Zeus Boulaios, 'Zeus of the Council/of council', and Athena Boulaia, 'Athena of the Council/of council' as they entered the chamber (Antiphon 6.45); we know that the same prayer and curse were uttered at the Assembly (Dem.19.70) and it is probable (if unprovable) that here too there was a preliminary sacrifice and purification. This ritual aspect must to some degree have been present in most if not all formal meetings of state bodies. And public office at all levels included religious functions. This is clearest in the case of the King-Archon, whose responsibilities (described on p. 82) were largely religious. But this is just the most prominent case. Many public officials were also required to make sacrifices on behalf of the city as a whole or their specific body and many, if not all, civic offices and functions involved the swearing of an oath.

This intersection between the political and the sacred can be seen from the opposite direction in the role of priests (and priestesses).

In Greece and Rome, priesthood was almost invariably a function rather than a vocation and the qualifications were usually formal (birth, age, gender, citizen and marital status). Some priesthoods were tied to a particular genos and remained so, since religious cults tend to be conservative, and for very good reasons; one cannot be sure what will provoke a god and it is safer not to meddle. But despite this element of conservatism, the religious activity of the city evolved and new cults were established throughout the life of the democracy. New priesthoods created in the mature democracy were generally filled by the polis or the deme, often by lot. We have an early example in the case of Myrrhine, the first priestess of Athena Nike ('victory') in the second half of the fifth century, whose epitaph proudly records:[3]

> Far-shining memorial of Kallimachos'
> daughter, who first
> tended the temple
> of Nike.
> She had a name
> companion to her good repute,
> as by divine fortune Myrrhine
> she was called
> in truth;
> she was first
> to tend the statue (?)
> of Athena Nike,
> (chosen) by lot from all,
> by good fortune.

Where a priest was appointed for a fixed term (as was often the case), he was like any other official of the city liable to audit on his conduct in office, *euthynai*, on expiry of his term.[4]

Another way in which religion visibly impacted on the administrative life of the city was in divination. The Greeks lived in a world which was full of signs, of the shape of future events, of divine will, divine favour or hostility, from the trivial to the momentous. Xenophon gives us a

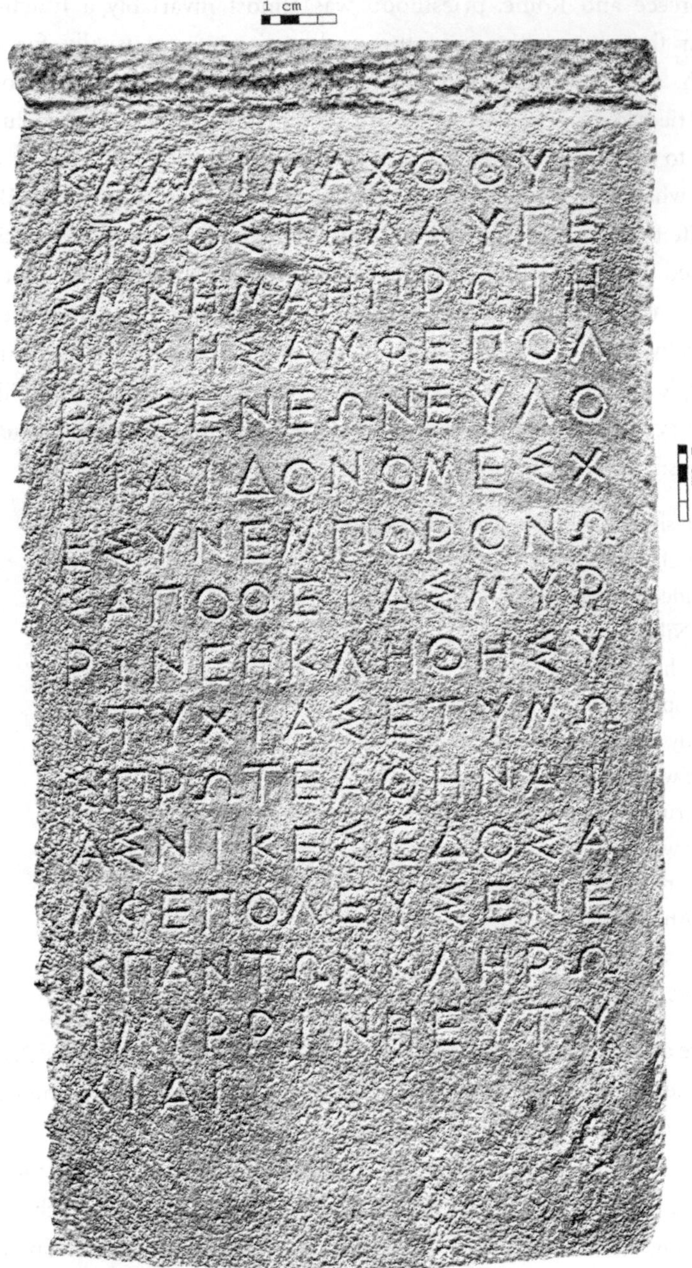

Figure 6.2 Epitaph of Myrrhine, priestess of Athene Nike.

partial list at *Memorabilia* 1.1.3 in defending Sokrates from the charge of introducing strange gods:

> He was no more introducing anything strange than are others who believe in divination and rely on birds, chance utterances, coincidences and sacrifices. For these don't suppose that the birds or the people they encounter know what is good for the inquirer, but that the gods make this known through them; and that was Sokrates' belief too.

The chorus of Aristophanes' *Birds* tell a similar story.[5]

Xenophon is talking about private divination by or for the individual. But divination also played an important role at polis level. It was an inbuilt feature of civic sacrifices, especially initiatory sacrifice before a meeting, a project, an expedition or a battle, since the state and behaviour of the victim, the entrails and the fire were searched for positive or negative signals. As well as sacrifice, bird signs and dreams figured as sources of knowledge and reassurance in civic as well as private life. Our fullest case of dream divination comes from a fascinating speech by the politician and speechwriter, Hypereides.[6] When Athens was awarded land at Oropos by Philip of Macedon after the battle of Chaironeia in 338, the land was parcelled out among the Athenian tribes. The status of part of the land was uncertain; some thought it belonged to the local god Amphiaraos. To settle the question three men were instructed to sleep in Amphiaraos' temple to seek a dream-sign from the god, a regular method both of divination and of healing. Political debate could also be swayed by the collections of prophesies (attributed to figures such as Bakis, Mousaios or the Sibyl) which had existed from the archaic period. Like the prophesies of Nostradamus, most of these were not explicitly tied to a particular time, place or event and so they could be brought out for examination and exploitation as circumstances allowed. Though anyone could attempt to interpret (as we see in Herodotos' account of the assembly debate about the oracle of the 'wooden walls' during the Persian invasion of 480[7]), there were people who claimed a special expertise in this task, the *chresmologoi*, 'oracle readers/collectors' (the Greek term is ambiguous).

Their prominence in public debate is rarely noted by our sources, who are more interested in the politicians and the people. But it can be seen from Aristophanes' *Birds*; when the hero creates his new city of the birds, one of the intruders who come to take advantage of the new foundation is explicitly identified as a *chresmologos*, who comes spouting oracles from Bakis, and like all such figures in Aristophanes is rudely rejected.[8] Here the *chresmologos* is dismissed as a mere nuisance. But the scale of the influence of divination on policy can be seen from the public reaction after the disaster in Sicily: the Athenians turned on everyone who had encouraged them to believe that they could succeed, not just the public speakers but 'also the oracle reciters and the prophets and all who with divination inspired them to believe they could take Sicily'.[9] This is all happening at a local level. But Athens (like other Greek cities) regularly consulted Panhellenic oracles, especially those at Delphi and Dodona, on any major civic venture.

One further area for divination needs to be mentioned: the army. Here Athens differed little, if at all, from any other Greek state, democratic or not. Rituals designed to secure divine favour accompanied the departure for war and battle and were always preceded by a sacrifice. Seers accompanied Greek armies on campaign. They performed the pre-battle sacrifice both to secure the goodwill of the gods and to determine the right moment to engage by inspecting the entrails of the victim. We can see the importance of their role from the grant of citizenship decreed by the Athenian demos after the battle of Knidos in 394 for a seer, Sthorys of Thasos, who had prophesied the victory from the offerings.[10]

Religion also played a part in the relentless political competition for influence which characterized Athenian political life. As we have seen already, charges of impiety are prominent among the public actions brought against politicians and their associates by opponents.[11] Religion is invaluable for this purpose. This is partly because of the crucial importance of the gods for the safety of the polis and the anxieties stirred by anything which might alienate them. These anxieties were most visibly in play during the twin scandals of the mutilation of the

Figure 6.3 Sacrifice of a boar.

Herms and the profanation of the Mysteries in 415, when Alkibiades' enemies used the collective anxieties to demolish his seemingly unassailable popularity.[12] But the ready recourse to prosecutions for impiety also reflects the complexities of ritual and cult, which opened space for error and offered a purchase for allegations of abuse. One such instance is preserved in [Demosthenes] 59.116:

> It is worthwhile, men of Athens, to bear this in mind too, that you punished Archias, who had served as Hierophant [i.e. the senior priest of the Elesusian Mysteries], when it was proved in court that he committed impiety by making sacrifice contrary to ancestral custom. Among the charges against him was that during the Haloa he sacrificed

for the courtesan Sinope a victim she brought on the hearth in the courtyard at Eleusis, though it is not permitted to sacrifice victims on that day, and the sacrifice was not his concern but the priestess's.

This looks like the playing out of policy divisions in court. Archias was almost certainly on the pro-Spartan side of one of the great foreign policy disputes of the early fourth century, whether alignment with Sparta or with Thebes best served Athens' interests. The other advantage of religious charges is that they open up an additional front for prosecution. Religion was the only area of public life where women played a significant role, and accusations of impiety made it possible to attack an opponent through his womenfolk. It is no coincidence that Aspasia, Perikles' mistress, figures among the associates charged with impiety by his enemies. Accusations of impiety also figure in the attack on the politician Stephanos through his mistress Neaira in [Demosthenes] 59.

This, however, is to focus too much on the direct interaction between religion and politics at the level of power, policy and administration. Above and beyond this more or less overtly political aspect of religion the worship of the gods and heroes was a constant presence embedded in Athenian public life, where it was an important factor both in uniting and in defining members of the polis.

At a very basic level, the cult topography of Athens is important for the sense of identity. The distribution of cult sites in Greek states help to define, demarcate and consolidate both territory and population; Athens was like other Greek states in this respect. Though many of the major cult sites were within Athens itself, there were major cults located across Attica, (including) from the panhellenic cult of Demeter and Kore west of Athens at Eleusis, about twenty kilometres from the border with Megara to the cults on the east coast, including Athena Pronoia at Prasiai, Artemis Tauropolos and Brauronia at Halai and at Brauron. There were also the cults of Amphiaraos and Nemesis to the north, near the border with Boiotia, at Oropos and Rhamnous, as well as those to Athena and Poseidon at Sounion on the southern tip of Attica. These sites are distinct from the many purely local cults operating in the individual demes. These locations both act as a counterweight to the inevitable importance of the city itself and help to sustain a sense of solidarity. They also demarcate Athenian space and complement the more practical role served by the border forts.

Religious activity is important for maintaining the goodwill of the gods. But it is not just a vertical phenomenon involving communication with superhuman forces above and below; it is also a horizontal construction creating and cementing social networks and relationships. In Athens, the sheer scale of formal cult activity meant that this aspect of religion was a constant and very visible presence. Thucydides' Perikles says of Athens:[13]

> we have created an abundance of release from toil for the mind, with regular competitions and sacrifices all year round . . .

The frank emphasis on the recreational value of festivals may surprise, less in the reference to games and competitions (a feature of many cults in the Greek world) than in the mention of sacrifice. But quite apart from the social aspect of collective ritual in any culture, sacrifice is especially important in a culture where meat may not be a frequent part of the diet, since one feature of animal sacrifice was that the bulk of the victim was shared among the worshippers. But the key point to note here is the emphasis on frequency. The religious calendar of Athens was densely packed. There was almost no month which had no major festival and many months had several, of which some lasted for two or more days. And the frequency was magnified by the existence of regular festivals in all the subgroups of the polis.

These festivals varied widely in kind and this variety itself contributes to the recreational aspect of cult activity noted by Perikles. A central feature of many was the procession (*pompe*) to the place of sacrifice, which like processions in many modern cultures involved active and organized participants, stragglers walking behind and large crowds of bystanders lining the route to watch, encourage and enjoy. We get a lively impression of such a procession from Dikaiopolis' private celebration of the Country Dionysia in Aristophanes' *Acharnians*:[14]

Come, daughter, see to it you carry the basket prettily, pretty,
with a savory-chewing face. Happy the man
who will bed you and sire – cats,
as good as you at – farting in the predawn light.
Step on, and in the crowd take great care
that someone doesn't sneakily nibble your jewellery.
Xanthias, your job is to hold straight
the phallos-pole behind the basket bearer.
I will follow and sing the phallic song.
And you, wife, watch me from the roof. On!

These processions could present an elaborate and splendid spectacle, as with the Panathenaic procession, so central a part of the goddess's cult that it was depicted on the Parthenon frieze. The Panathenaic procession was a profoundly political act (in the widest sense). Members of the whole population (not just the citizen body) took part in the parade, divided into different groups, and the citizen body was also subdivided for the procession by age and military role. It was a process which visually united and defined the whole population. Since this event took place in midsummer, in Hekatombaion, the first month of the Athenian year, it offered a spectacular start to the year, enhanced by the role in the procession of the *peplos*, the new robe woven for the goddess's statue, which served as the sail of a massive ship on wheels. The Anthesteria, a winter festival for Dionysos, also featured a ship on wheels which brought the god to the city. The length of the route was also an important part of the event in creating a sense of the sacral and civic importance of the ritual. In the case of the Panathenaia, the procession began at the Dipylon Gate and wound south through the Kerameikos, crossing the Agora diagonally eastwards before turning west to ascend to the Acropolis, creating a long, slow build up to the moment of arrival and an opportunity for a large proportion of the population to view the event.[15]

As well as securing divine favour and bringing together the population, citizen and non-citizen, these festivals (like many secular aspects of Athenian life) rehearsed the distinctive status of the citizen within the community. The officiating roles were always taken by

Figure 6.4 Remains of the Athenian Agora looking toward the Acropolis.

citizens. And though metics participated in the Panathenaic procession, they were distinguished by purple robes and (like other participants) they marched in a distinct group; the procession thus recognized and honoured their position as inhabitants of Attica and simultaneously noted the status difference between them and the citizen participants.

Perikles also notes the ubiquitous presence of competitions. Greek gods as anthropomorphic beings shared not just human form but also human drives and tastes. Competition in various forms provided the gods with both a source of pleasure and also honour (by offering them the finest achievements of the human body and mind). They also offered a constant source of entertainment for human participants. But as well as the entertainment value many of the competitions involved a very high level of citizen participation as performers; in this respect religion replicates the emphasis on participation in secular politics. This is especially clear in the choral competitions which featured in many festivals, where competition was between tribes either singly or in pairs. Choral activity was a Greek and not just an Athenian phenomenon. But the number of tribes at Athens made for choral events on a scale probably unrivalled in any other Greek city and exceeded only by the big Panhellenic gatherings at the major Greek cult sites. The number of citizens mobilized in these competitions is remarkable for the size of the citizen population. At the City Dionysia festival, each tribe offered a chorus of grown men and a chorus of boys. Each chorus had fifty members, giving us a total of 500 adult males and 500 boys. In addition, three tragic poets competed, as did five comic poets. The tragic chorus had fifteen members (from the time of Sophokles onward), the comic chorus twenty-four. This gives 120 comic choristers and thirty-six tragic choristers. We thus have roughly 1,150 choristers overall. To these we have to add the penumbra of support from stagehands. For the individuals involved the impact was considerable, since time was needed for rehearsal. The importance attached to this by the polis can be gauged by the fact that performers and producers had exemption from military service to ensure that they could attend rehearsals and the festival, perhaps more strikingly by the fact that prisoners were let out of jail for the festival.[16]

Religion was also important for status definition in relation to females. Some festivals were exclusive to women and of these some seem to have been open to all women. But some festivals such as the Thesmophoria, which forms the location for Aristophanes' *Women at the Thesmophoria*, were exclusive to citizen women. As often with women's festivals, this had a pronounced emphasis on fertility. But the restriction to citizen women made it an important status marker. In this respect Athenian religion complemented the secular boundaries created by the exclusivity of Athenian marriage law.[17] This aspect of cult is still clearer in the ceremonies at Brauron on the coast in honour of Artemis, which were a kind of rite of passage for citizen girls (or at least for a representative selection of them), in which girls danced the part of bears. The chorus of Aristophanes' *Lysistrata* (641–7), in claiming the right to speak to the city, describe a sequence of rituals acts they have performed, among them (643): 'Then wearing my saphron robe I was a bear at the Brauronia.'

Perhaps the most striking example of the intersection of the political and the sacred in relation to women is the role of the Basilinna, the wife of the King-Archon, in the Anthesteria, a three-day winter festival in honour of Dionysos. On the second day, the Basilinna was given in marriage to the god Dionysos.[18] The presence of Dionysos and marriage point to a ritual designed to secure fertility, though the location in the heart of the city (in the old Agora, for which see p. 118) suggests that this is not just about the fertility of crops and animals but also human fertility and the continuation of the polis. The choice of the wife of the Basileus coheres with his predominantly ritual role (p. 82), but the specific choice of the wife of an official neatly underscores the degree to which religion is embedded in the administrative and political life of the polis.

The role of cult in sustaining the sense of identity was replicated at the level of genos, phratry and deme. Admission to the phratry took place at the Apatouria, the main festival of the phratries, and was accompanied by offerings. Since membership of phratry and genos was confined to males of citizen status, this and the other festivals again had the effect of rehearsing the unique position of the Athenian citizen. The demes, also like the polis, had their own cults and organized their own festivals. With 139 demes this gives Athens an exceptional scale of sub-polis cult activity and confirms Perikles' claim in Thucydides. Again as with the polis, non-citizens could sometimes participate on an equal footing. But this was not inevitable and the citizen deme members remained a privileged group within the deme's cultic activity. And again the administration of cults at deme (as at state) level was in the hands of the deme assembly and the deme officials. This included selection of and eligibility for priesthoods. The speaker of Demosthenes 57 cites as evidence of his citizen status the fact that he was balloted by his deme (Halimous) for the appointment to the (local) priesthood of Herakles.[19]

There is one final level where religion matters for city and citizens. So far we have been looking at religion within the city, but there is also a wider Greek context. Religion played a part in Athenian control over the empire in the fifth century; subject allies were required both to contribute to and to participate in the major Athenian or (like Eleusis) Athenian-controlled festivals. And both before and after the democracy

Athens, like other Greek states, sent delegations to major Greek shrines and locations to participate in Panhellenic cults. The general term for this kind of external cult participation is *theoria*. The occasions included the four major Greek athletic festivals (the Olympic, Pythian, Isthmian and Nemean Games), where as well as athletes travelling to compete there were also groups of *theoroi* sent to offer sacrifice to the god. They also included the island of Delos, dominated by Athens long after the fifth-century empire. These delegations, especially at Delos and Delphi, would often include choral performances in honour of the god of the sanctuary. The groups of representatives could therefore be very large. As well as displaying the piety of the polis to the world of Greece, these occasions offered an opportunity for cultural competition and display (where they involved choral song and dance) to complement the display at the Dionysia for those visiting the city (p. 131). Like any modern international gathering, they also offered an opportunity for various kinds of diplomatic activity. The interplay between politics and piety in relation to the Panhellenic sanctuaries is perhaps most visible in the role of Delos as the centre (and treasury) of the anti-Persian alliance (the Delian League) created by Athens after the defeat of the second Persian invasion of 480. But it is a constant presence in Greek history. For instance, the Amphictyonic Council, a consortium of states which oversaw the shrine at Delphi, and to whose meetings Athens sent two delegates, became the focus of fierce interstate competition in the middle of the fourth century, firstly when friction between Phokis and Thebes led to the outbreak of the Third Sacred War in 356 and then in 346 when Philip of Macedon, having resolved the war, was allocated the seats previously reserved for the defeated Phokis and invited to preside at the Pythian Games. This caused a serious crisis for Athens as Phokis' ally: Athens had to choose between refusing to recognize Philip's place on the council and boycotting the games, which might have provoked hostilities with the Amphictyonic states collectively, or participating at the humiliating cost of seeing Philip triumphant. Pragmatism prevailed.[20]

7

Local Government: The Demes

The demes were the building blocks of Athenian democracy. The deme was central to the identity of an Athenian citizen, whose full title was name, father's name and demotic: 'Demosthenes son of Demosthenes of the deme Paiania' (*Demosthenes Demosthenous Paianieus*). Entitlement to deme membership was based on the place of residence of paternal ancestors at the time of Kleisthenes' reforms. Though there was a strong link between deme membership and residence, not all deme members lived in the deme. Hence the speaker of Demosthenes 57, explaining why members slipped away from an extraordinary meeting of the deme Halimous held in Athens, finds it useful to explain:[1]

> I was roughly sixtieth, and I was called last of all those who were called on that day, when the older demesmen had gone off to the country; for since our deme, jurors, is thirty-five stades [about 6.5 km] from the city and most members live there, the majority had gone off, and those who remained were no more than thirty.

The demes varied enormously in size, as we can see from the lists of Council members returned from each deme, ranging from Acharnai, which returned twenty-two members, to small villages, which returned one or two.

The demes were essential to the functioning of the polis. At the most basic level, it was through membership of the deme that an Athenian acquired his citizen rights. Only when he had been accepted by his deme at his *dokimasia* at eighteen and had his name entered on the deme register could an Athenian exercise the full rights of a citizen. In addition to the regular scrutiny of new members, the demes were used at least twice for a procedure of extraordinary scrutiny (*diapsephis*) during the classical period; the first was in 445/4 after a gift of grain from Egypt was distributed among the citizen population; the second was in 346/5.[2] On each occasion the deme voted on each member in turn. Both scrutinies removed substantial numbers from the deme lists.

The demes also played a part in the filling of some posts in the city administration. Council membership was based not just on tribe but on deme. The demes also played a part in the selection of public arbitrators.[3] At some (unspecified) period the demes had played a role in the pre-selection of candidates for offices selected by lot, but by the 320s this had been abandoned because of problems with corruption.[4]

But the demes were more than a mechanism to facilitate the central administration. They also had a political life of their own and were important for local government. In many respects their structures and activities, which were put in place by Kleisthenes, mirrored those of the city. Like the city, each deme had its own assembly, called the agora (the term *ekklesia* was reserved for meetings of the state Assembly on the Pnyx), which met as required. All adult male members of the deme were eligible to attend meetings, which were conducted like the Athenian Assembly, with formal proposals which were then inscribed on stone as deme decrees. Like the decrees of the Athenian Assembly, those of the demes ranged from practical business to formal bestowal of honours. The deme assembly business included the election of deme officials, who like state officials were subject to a *dokimasia* before serving and *euthynai* on leaving office.[5] Like the state, the demes owned land, which would be leased out. As we have seen, they also had their own cults and festivals.[6] For the financing of some aspects of these, they imposed liturgies. A speaker in Isaios lists the duty of feasting the women of the deme at the deme Thesmophoria among the liturgies falling on richer members within the deme.[7] The financial activity of some demes at least involved the charging of a tax (*enktetikon*) on non-members owning land in the deme.

In one important respect the demes and the city operated as separate spheres. We might expect the aspiring politician to use local government to hone his political and administrative skills before moving on to participate in state politics, as happens in some modern democracies.

But as far as we can tell, individuals who played a prominent part in deme politics were not prominent in politics at the polis level.

The principal official of the deme was the demarch (*demarchos*), selected by lot, who combined the modern roles of mayor and chief executive of a borough council. The demarch also had control over the deme register. He presided over meetings of the deme assembly. It was the demarch's job to pursue anyone defaulting on rents due to the deme.[8] He participated in the organization of deme cults and in some cases offered sacrifices, in line with the normal convergence between religious and secular activities in Greece. His responsibilities in the area of religion extended to ensuring that those who died in the deme were buried by their relatives, or, if none could be found, contracting out the task on behalf of the deme.[9] He would represent the deme in any court cases (except those arising from appeals against the annual *dokimasia* of new members, when the deme elected five members to act for it[10]).

Though we can construct a model for the broad operation of the demes, in practice they differed significantly in the efficiency with which they conducted their business. The speaker of Demosthenes 57 claims that at one point early in the fourth century, the register of the deme Halimous was lost and the deme members had to reconstruct it by holding a special vote on all their members to check eligibility.[11] The speaker is a man with a grudge against his deme, and so we cannot assume that he is telling the truth. But the fact that the allegation could be made suggests that the Athenians themselves accepted that local government in Athens (as in many modern democracies, including Britain) varied enormously in quality. The two state-wide special scrutinies of deme members testify to a degree of suspicion about the consistency of administrative standards across the demes. We learn from the entry under *Potamos* in the lexicographer Harpocration that the deme *Potamos* in particular (rightly or wrongly) was notorious for its casual approach to the admission of new members.

8

The Democratic Landscape

Though I have focused so far on institutions, roles and practices, these do not exist in a physical vacuum. The cityscape within which the democracy functions is also important, since as well as defining political processes at a practical level, it also by location, layout and structure reflects, shapes or consolidates the sense of civic identity. To gain this concrete sense of democracy in operation, we need to walk the ancient city.

We begin our mental tour of Athens in the Agora, north-west of the Acropolis (Figures 5.1, 6.1, 8.1). This part of the city did not acquire a civic role until the late archaic period. In the late Bronze Age and through the dark ages following the fall of the Mycenaean palace

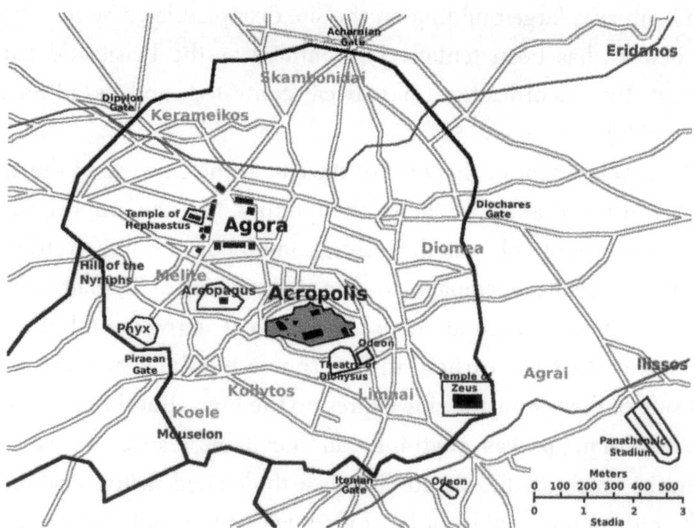

Figure 8.1 Athens, showing the Agora, Pnyx, Areiopagos and Acropolis.

kingdoms, it was used partly for private habitation, partly as a burial ground. Only in the sixth century did public buildings begin to appear, possibly at the very end of the century after the reforms of Kleisthenes. Research over the last two decades makes it almost certain that the pre-classical Agora was just to the north of the east end of the Acropolis, that is, east and south of the area we now know as the Agora. We can, however, see evidence for a serious attempt to give the area which became the classical Agora a focal role under the sixth-century tyranny. The altar of the Twelve Gods set up in what became the classical Agora by Peisistratos (grandson of the tyrant) in the 520s[1] was used as early as the fifth century as the starting point for measurements of distance from Athens to other parts of the territory, which indicates an acceptance that it was physically the centre point of Attica, and this may have been its intended role from the outset. The building of the fountain-house in the south-east part of the Agora, datable to the last quarter of the sixth century, complements this development by siting a major public utility in the vicinity. The interest of the tyrants in this area may reflect the location of their own palace. One of the structures on the west side certainly datable to the second half of the sixth century, a large building on the site occupied later by the Tholos (see below), has been tentatively identified as the Peisitratid palace (though the identification has been contested and is ultimately unprovable).

The development of this part of the city at the expense of the older Agora continued after the fall of the tyranny. The new importance of the popular Assembly on the Pnyx, combined with the continuing importance of the Areiopagos before the reforms of Ephialtes, made these two hills a natural focus for political activity, and it is no coincidence that the earliest administrative buildings appear on the west side of the Agora, the side nearest to the Pnyx. But though natural, this development was anything but inevitable, especially as some functions (such as the sacred civic hearth, located in the Prytaneion in the old Agora) could not be shifted, with the result that there was some duplication of role between buildings in the old and new Agoras.

Relocation of the civic centre in this way is very unusual. As the steady accumulation of buildings in the area indicates, this is deliberate policy, not urban planning drift. It represents a conscious break with the past, almost like a refounding of the city, and shows remarkable confidence on the part of the new regime.

The term agora is used in two senses. The word means (among other things) 'market' and is used to designate the central retail area of the city. In this larger sense the term agora covered the commercial premises situated in the large square and spilling over into neighbouring streets (there were also shops elsewhere in the city) and beyond the city walls immediately to the north-west. There were not just shops but also movable stalls, which probably covered much of the empty space in the centre of the square, very much like modern markets, and (at the bottom end of the commercial ladder) people like the sausage-seller in Aristophanes' *Knights* selling from portable trays.[2]

But the term was also used to designate a clearly defined area marked out by boundary stones (inscribed 'I am the boundary of the Agora') which served as the civic centre of the city. The Agora in this narrower sense was sacred, and there were containers of water at certain points for those entering the area to cleanse themselves. The civic buildings and activities within this zone had a religious as well as a political significance. Accordingly, those who were unclean (such as those accused of homicide) were barred from the Agora. The bar on entry to this area went beyond religious scruple, however. This was the heart of the city, and entry into the Agora was a privilege. Athenian citizens who had forfeited their citizen rights were barred from entering the Agora.

On the west side of the square, below the low hill of Kolonos on which the temple to Hephaistos stands, about halfway down the west side of the Agora, stood the Council Chamber (*Bouleuterion*). There were actually two Council buildings. Little remains of the older council building, which is commonly dated to about 500, immediately after the reforms of Kleisthenes. It appears to have had an anteroom on the south side with the larger meeting room occupying about two

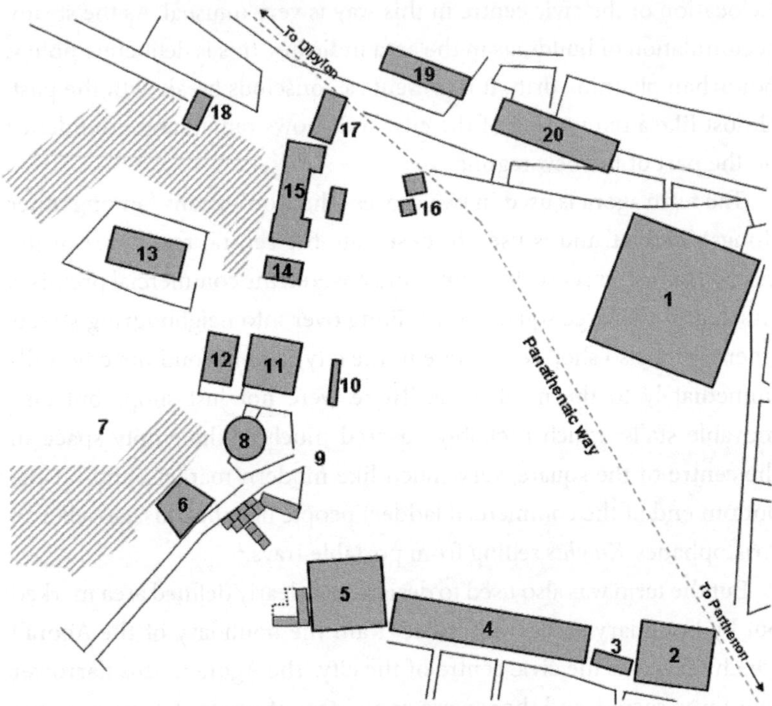

Figure 8.2 The Agora at the end of the fifth century.

Key

1 Court
2 Mint
3 Enneakrounos (Nine-spout well)
4 South Stoa
5 Aiakeion
6 Strategeion
7 Kolonos Agoraios (raised area to the west of the Agora)
8 Tholos
9 Agora stone
10 Statues of the Eponymous Heroes
11 Metroon (Old Bouleuterion)
12 New Bouleuterion
13 Temple of Hephaistos
14 Temple of Apollo Patroos
15 Stoa of Zeus
16 Altar of the Twelve Gods
17 Stoa Basileios (Royal stoa)
18 Temple of Aphrodite Ourania
19 Stoa of Hermes
20 Stoa Poikile

thirds of the site. This building was superseded in the last two decades of the fifth century by a new Council Chamber, which was built immediately behind it. The Old Bouleuterion was not demolished but served as the sanctuary to the Mother of the Gods, hence its name, the *Metroon* ('mother's shrine'). It was here that in the last decade of the fifth century the Athenians created an archive of legal statutes. Immediately to the south stood the Tholos. This was the building which housed the standing committee of the Council of 500, the Boule.

The Council Chamber, both new and old, had a sacral character. There were divine statues there (the later traveller Pausanias mentions statues of Demos, the people personified, Apollo and Zeus Bouliaios, Zeus of the Council). There was also a hearth, which again was sacred. It was here that Theramenes took refuge in 403 when under threat from Kritias as the oligarchy of the Thirty fragmented. Theramenes was dragged off by the Scythian archers, in what was for the Greeks a shocking act of sacrilege.[3]

In front of the Metroon during the fourth century (earlier their position may have been further south) stood the statues of the eponymous heroes, that is, the heroes after whom the ten tribes created by Kleisthenes were named. Their location within the Agora probably reflects a desire after Kleisthenes' reforms to give prominence to the new tribal system. These statues figure quite prominently in our literary sources. This is not a matter of aesthetics or religion, but rather reflects the public role played by the statues in the communications system of ancient Athens. The statues served as a place for posting public notices. We know, for instance, that when there was to be a military campaign, the names of those required for service were posted by the statues of the eponymous heroes. Aristophanes gives us a vivid account of the individual response to this notice:[4]

> The expedition leaves tomorrow.
> But he hasn't bought his provisions – he didn't know he was going.
> Then standing by the statue of Pandion he sees his name
> and dumbfounded at the disaster he runs off with a look like vinegar.

The statues were also used for posting notice of lawsuits. Under the fourth-century procedures for legislation, we find provision for draft statutes to be placed for inspection in front of the statues of the heroes to allow consultation in advance of the relevant Assembly meeting.

Immediately to the south of the Old Bouleuterion was a round building known as the Tholos. Its shape is still clearly visible in the Agora excavations. This building served as the headquarters of the Prytaneis, the executive committee of the Council. It was in the Tholos that the Prytaneis used to dine at state expense. Part of their number slept there so that there was always a contingent of the Council on duty in case of emergency. Fragments of crockery probably used at the Tholos have been found. These are marked with the letters ΔH (delta eta), short for *demosios*, 'public property', to prevent members of the Prytaneis from absent-mindedly taking the crockery home for their personal use.

Other offices have been conjecturally located near the Council complex, though it is difficult to fix their sites with precision. Somewhere in the south-west corner of the Agora may have stood the offices of the 'Sellers', *poletai*, (the location is conjectural, based on inscriptional finds in the area).[5] The location near the Council complex makes sense, given

Figure 8.3 Remains of the monument of the eponymous heroes.

the importance of the Council for the financial administration of the state. The office of the generals, the *Strategeion* (from *strategos*, 'general'), has been conjecturally located (again on the basis of inscriptional finds) in the same area. One can feel a little more confident about the office of the cavalry commanders (the *Hipparcheion*). Inscriptional and other finds suggest that it belongs somewhere in the north-west corner of the Agora. Again the location within easy reach of the Bouleuterion makes sense, since the Council annually vetted the fitness and the treatment of the horses, the fitness of the cavalrymen and their financial ability to maintain a horse.[6] Just beyond the south-west corner of the Agora, on the way to the Pnyx, are the remains of a building which has been conjecturally identified as the Athenian state prison. Its modest scale reflects the fact that prison in Athens was not in itself a form of punishment but a temporary measure. The location close to the lawcourts (many of which were in the Agora) makes sense, since the prison served as among other things a holding pen for anyone held in custody pending trial or payment of fine or (like Sokrates) the enactment of penalty.

There are several other buildings we need to consider before we leave the Agora. By the end of the fifth century there were a number of porticoes (Greek, *stoa*), open-sided structures affording shelter from sun and rain, on the edge of the Agora. On the west side, north of the Bouleuterion, were the Stoa of Zeus the Liberator (Zeus Eleutherios; built in the second half of the century), and the Royal Stoa (Stoa Basileios). The Royal Stoa was associated with the King-Archon. We know that this stoa was occasionally used as a venue for the court of the Areiopagos (over which the King-Archon presided). It was in the Royal Stoa that the stone tablets bearing the reinscribed laws were set up at the end of the fifth century. On the north side was the Stoa of the Herms and the Stoa Poikile (Painted Portico). There was yet another stoa on the south side of the Agora. The south stoa may have served as the base for several boards of magistrates. Two offices we would expect to find in the Agora are those of the market officials (*agoranomoi, metronomoi* – see p. 80), and an inscription of the *metronomoi* (from the third century) found in the south stoa makes this a good bet. The location would be consistent with its proximity to a building in the south-east corner of the Agora which has been identified on the basis of finds as the Athenian mint.

The Stoa Poikile is worth a moment's pause before we move on. It was built toward the middle of the fifth century and derived its name from the paintings by celebrated artists which adorned the walls. The pictures had a profoundly political character (in the broadest sense): they celebrated Athenian military achievements, directly or indirectly. One painting depicted Marathon and was matched by pictures of the battle of Theseus against the Amazons and the sack of Troy; this both heroized the Persian Wars and located them in the context of a tradition of east–west hostility. But we know that another picture depicted a battle against Sparta and it was here that the Athenians dedicated the shields taken from the Spartans at Pylos. One of these survives and is now in the Agora Museum. It reads 'The Athenians from the Spartans from Pylos', i.e. 'the Athenians dedicated this shield out of the spoils from the Spartans taken at Pylos' (dedications are commonly abbreviated in this way). The building was also used as a lawcourt.

This brings us to another important aspect of the Agora. So far we have largely been looking at the Agora as an administrative centre. But it was also the focal point for judicial activities. There was no single lawcourt in Athens but many. To run the legal system, the city needed a range of buildings of different sizes. We know the names of a number of lawcourts but it is difficult to identify them with confidence. Part of the problem is that the buildings used as courts were not necessarily distinguished architecturally. Those that were (such as the Stoa Poikile and the Odeion next to the Theatre of Dionysos) were not exclusively lawcourts but served multiple civic purposes. There was a large building in the south-west corner of the Agora which has traditionally been designated 'Heliaia', that is, one of the largest courts; unfortunately recent research suggests that, though it was to some degree connected with legal and administrative activities, it may not have been a

Figure 8.4 Shield dedicated after the capture of the Spartans at Pylos, now in the Agora Museum at Athens.

court. One can be more confident about the building in the north-east corner, where voting ballots were found of a sort described as used in the fourth century, that is, discs pierced with a short rod, a hollow rod for conviction, a solid rod for acquittal. Two other important pieces of court furniture have been found in the Agora. The first is an allotment machine (*kleroterion*) used in the fourth century to select jurors for the day and allocate them to courts. The second is a water-clock (*klepsydra*), a crude but effective device consisting of a pot with a hole at the base. The hole could be stopped with a bung. The pot was filled with water and when the trial began, the bung was removed. The amount of water (and so the number of pots) allowed varied according to the importance of the type of case; when the water ran out, the speaker had to stop. Though we can use this device to calculate the time allowed for cases in classical Athens, we do not know for certain that it is identical with the containers used in court, since it is inscribed with the name of the tribe Antiochis, not designated as city property.

If we leave the Agora by the south-west corner, we come to two adjacent hills which between them map out the constitutional history of fifth-century Athens: the Pnyx and the Areiopagos.

The Areiopagos site reveals little of its historical importance. The key political site of democratic Athens was the adjacent hill of the Pnyx, the regular site for meetings of the Assembly. Unlike the Areiopagos, the Pnyx reveals a lot about its history. Although only citizens could

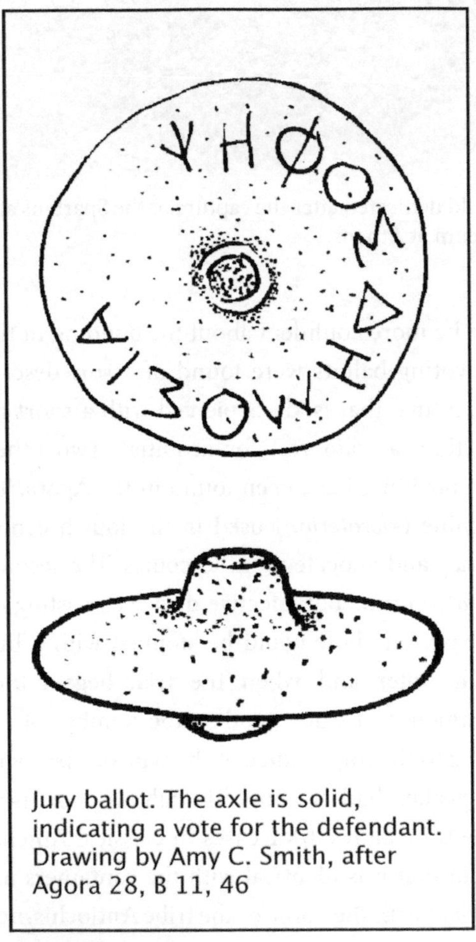

Jury ballot. The axle is solid, indicating a vote for the defendant. Drawing by Amy C. Smith, after Agora 28, B 11, 46

Figure 8.5 Jurors' ballots.

Figure 8.6 Remains of the kleroterion ('allotment') machines for allocating jurors to courts.

participate, there was space for outsiders to observe proceedings. The audience sat on the ground in a banked auditorium. The speakers addressed them from a raised rostrum (the *bema*). During the fifth century, the natural contours of the hill dictated the orientation of the site; the audience faced north and the speakers' platform faced south. Around 400 there was a major reconstruction of the site and the positions were reversed, as we know both from literary and from archaeological evidence. Our literary source ascribes the change to the Thirty and explains it as an ideological move: the speakers' platform was turned from the sea, associated with the navy and democracy, to face the land.[7] The date of the reorientation has been contested. But a more plausible explanation irrespective of the date is that the intention was to shelter the audience from the wind. In fact, from the end of the sixth century Athens had a capacious auditorium with good shelter from the wind, the Theatre of Dionysos on the southern slope of the

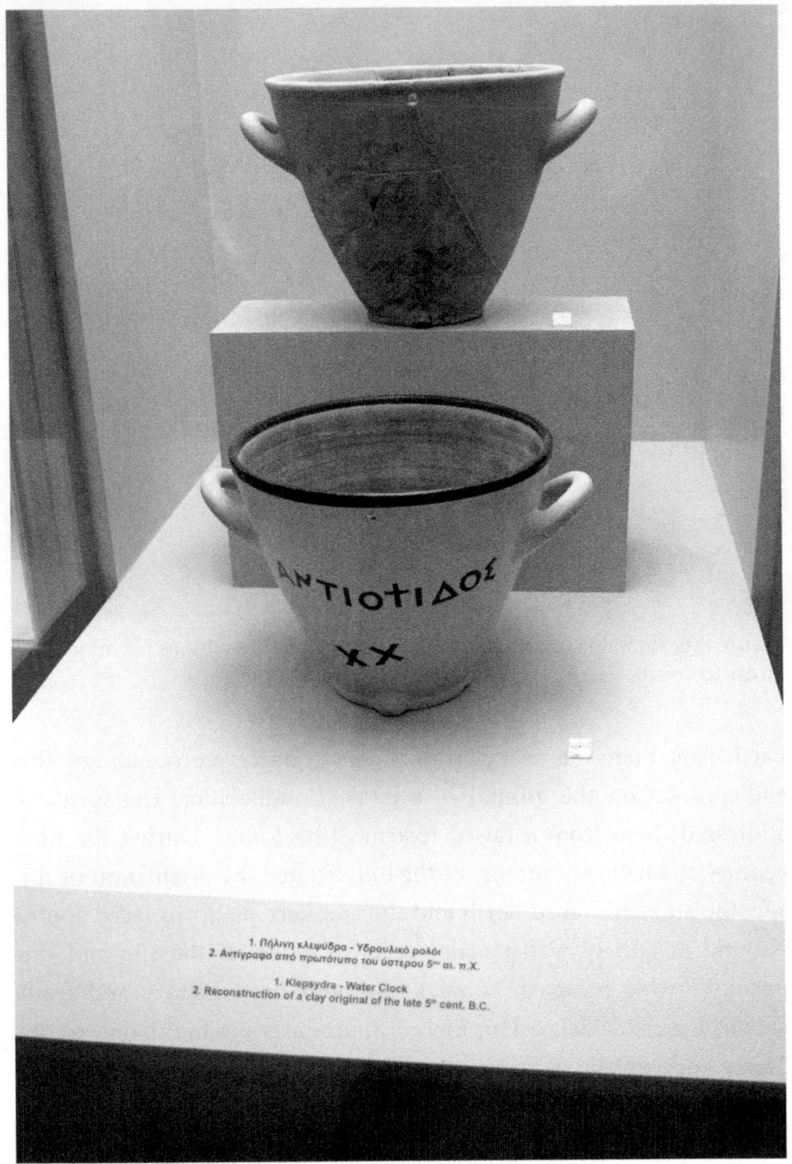

Figure 8.7 The klepsydra or waterclock (reconstruction).

Acropolis, which would have been an ideal location for the assembly. But this location was rarely used in the classical period. The Assembly regularly met there after the Dionysia in the spring to discuss the conduct of the festival[8] and (by the 320s) there was a further meeting at which the ephebes[9] gave a military display.[10] But the Pnyx was so obviously the proper location for the Assembly that in Aristophanes' *Knights* the personification of the Athenian people, Demos, is given as his deme-title, 'Demos Pyknites', 'Demos of Pnyx'.[11] Possibly, as has been suggested, the reluctance to move is in part due to conservatism, and in part due to the significance of the position; the hill was close to the Agora, the civic centre of Athens. The conservatism has a religious dimension, since as we have seen Assembly meetings were religious as well as secular occasions.

Directly east of the Pnyx is the Propylaia, the monumental entrance to the Acropolis. Though (according to Thucydides) the Acropolis had once (with the area immediately to the south) been the whole city, it was never in the classical period either inhabited or used as an

Figure 8.8 The speakers' platform (*bema*) on the Pnyx, late fourth century.

administrative centre. It was always given over to cult use. So the whole site had to be kept ritually pure. This is best illustrated by two scenes in Aristophanes' *Lysistrata*. When Myrrhine, one of the women who have seized the Acropolis as part of the sex strike, teases her husband with the promise of sex, one of her ploys to keep him at bay is to ask him how she is to purify herself. When the women, desperate for sex, try to escape from the Acropolis which they have seized, one of them claims to be pregnant.[12] Sex and childbirth alike leave the participant ritually unclean. The Acropolis was the end point of the most significant procession in the Athenian calendar, the Panathenaia. The Acropolis was of course the best defensive position in Athens and for this reason (as well as because it contained the treasury of Athena) it is the site seized by the women in Aristophanes' *Lysistrata*, as it had (in reality) been seized by Kylon and his co-conspirators in the late seventh century and by the Spartan forces of Kleomenes in the late sixth century. But beyond its practical political importance, the Acropolis and its buildings had a symbolic political aspect. The orator Aischines (writing in the middle of the fourth century) gives us an idea of this symbolic value when he talks about the debate which led to the conclusion of peace with Macedon in 346. He represents the speakers who opposed peace as appealing to Athens' great past. But the way they expressed themselves is revealing. At least according to Aischines, they urged the Assembly to look to the Propylaia, which all present could see simply by turning their heads and looking due east. In the same speech Aischines claims that the Theban general Epameinondas had proposed to set the Athenian Propylaia on the Kadmeia, that is, the Theban citadel.[13] The claim may be invention. But the symbolism is clear: the Propylaia here stands for Athens' role as one of the dominant cities of Greece.

Tucked into the south-east side of the Acropolis is the theatre of Dionysos. Though Athenian drama never had a formal political role, it was by definition *politikos*, 'of the polis', by its location within the annual state festivals. The dramatic festivals vividly illustrate the convergence of religious and secular in the ancient Greek polis. Their importance can be seen in the introduction during the fourth century of the theoric

Figure 8.9 The Propylaia and Acropolis viewed from the Pnyx.

payments to ensure a large citizen presence.[14] The principle festival for tragedy, the City Dionysia, was held in spring, when there would be a large number of foreigners in Athens. We know (from the fact that Athens was exporting tragedy as early as Aischylos) that Athenian tragedy was much admired outside the city's borders. The festival, in particular the theatrical spectacle, was therefore at one level a sustained display of Athenian cultural pre-eminence. The Athenians exploited this presence to make the festival an exercise in propaganda. It was at this time of the year that the members of the Athenian empire would bring the tribute in the fifth century, and we are told that the tribute was displayed in the theatre.[15] Grants of honours to citizens and foreigners were sometimes announced in the theatre. And it was here that the orphans of Athenians killed in war would parade on reaching maturity to receive the blessing of the demos and a gift of armour.[16] The festival thus displayed to the Greek world the wealth, power and prestige of Athens, the public spirit of her citizens, and the readiness of the demos to repay this, as well as the status of Athens as the artistic centre of

Greece. But the use of the theatre as a showcase survived the loss of the empire. This was not just propaganda for external purposes; like other ritual moments, the dramatic festivals are a celebration of Athenian identity. Within this context the tragedians often respond indirectly to contemporary events through the distancing medium of myth, providing another forum for the discussion of issues of concern. Unlike the Assembly, where the audience had to make hard decisions on thorny and sometimes urgent questions of policy, the theatre (where it did address political issues) allowed room for more detached exploration of concerns and thus for discordant voices sometimes out of step with collective ideology.

Unlike tragedy, comedy (in the fifth and early fourth century and intermittently afterwards) engages directly with contemporary politics. In general comedy focuses not on policy but on personalities and style. The prominent political figures are mercilessly satirized, either in

Figure 8.10 The theatre of Dionysos.

passing or as the target of whole plays. Though we tend to see, and admire, Perikles through Thucydides' eyes, we know that he was mocked ceaselessly by the comic poets; and as each of his successors – Kleon, Hyperbolos and Kleophon – became the dominant figure on the Pnyx, he was singled out for lampoon by the comic stage. It is impossible to tell in most cases how far the satire represents the poet's own views. But since the dramatists were in competition for popular favour, the recurrent attacks on leading politicians presumably reflect what the audience enjoyed. We are faced, therefore, with the paradox that the Athenians simultaneously gave influence and prestige and mocked its recipients. It has been suggested that the fifth-century theatre audience was more wealthy, and possibly more hostile to the demagogues, than the Assembly. The suggestion is based on the cost of attendance, which for a family would be expensive over the several days of the festival. But this is to ignore the importance of the festival and therefore the likelihood that people would save in order to attend, especially as it was only an annual event. It has also been pointed out that we do not know when the Athenians started charging for attendance at the theatre. There is no objective evidence that the citizens in the theatre audience differed significantly from the Assembly in their attitudes in the fifth century. So the paradox remains. Nowhere is this more visible than in the case of Kleon, who was lampooned by Aristophanes in a play (*Knights*) which won him first prize, but elected general very shortly afterwards. In part this paradox perhaps reflects the resentment arising within a political system which gave political control to the masses but gave political initiative, and substantial rewards, to elite politicians. But it also points to a practical purpose served by comedy. It helped to keep politicians in their place by reminding them where power ultimately lay; as such, it supplemented the more formal means of democratic control. This role for comedy as a means of democratic control is recognized by the Old Oligarch:[17] 'They do not allow ridicule and abuse of the *demos*, to avoid being criticized themselves, but in the case of individuals they encourage anyone who wishes, in the firm knowledge that the individual ridiculed is not as a rule one of the *demos* or the mass but someone with wealth or good birth or power. Very few poor people or members of the *demos* are ridiculed, and these only if they make a nuisance of themselves or seek to have more than the *demos*.' Though the author oversimplifies (the demos is occasionally a comic target, most notably in Aristophanes' *Knights*), he accurately grasps the relationship between informal and formal control of men of influence by the demos.

Next to the theatre stood the Odeion of Perikles, a large square structure supported on pillars. As well as serving as a hall for various purposes, like many large halls in Athens it served as a court room and is attested as such by the 420s.

To the south-east of the theatre stood another two buildings which have been identified tentatively with courts, the Palladion and the Delphinion. These were two of the homicide courts. Athenian homicide procedures allocated cases to courts according to factors such as the nature of the charge, the nature of the defence and the status of the victim. The Delphinion was the court used when the accused admitted homicide but claims the act was justified, while the Palladion tried cases where people were charged with involuntary homicide or causing death through an intermediary, or if the victim was a slave or a metic or a foreigner.

The final stop on our tour is the Kerameikos (from *kerameus*, 'potter'), the area immediately to the north of the Agora, stretching perhaps as far as the Academy (the precinct of the hero Akademos), 1.5 km to the north of the city. The Kerameikos was split in two by the expansion of the circuit of the walls by Themistokles after the second Persian invasion. It is the part outside the walls which concerns us here. To the modern tourist the Kerameikos is a cemetery but this simply reflects the fact that the prominent monuments which survive are tombs. In classical times, like most parts of the city this district had a number of functions, residential, manufacturing, retail, pleasure (we have literary and archaeological evidence for brothels there). But it was also a site for burial. From the end of the sixth century, burials within the city walls become very rare. There is evidence that burial within the city was not allowed. As a result, graves tend to lie outside the walls, on the roads leading away from the gates. The choice of site reflects both a desire for visibility and a need for accessibility. The dead were not cut off from the family. Families continued to make annual offerings to their dead, and proximity to a road made this much easier. The Kerameikos was an inevitable site for burials, as one of the major approaches to the city by land; two roads left the city here, through the Sacred Gate and the neighbouring Dipylon (double) Gate (known in the classical period as the Thriasian Gate).

The Kerameikos was not the only burial area in ancient Athens, but it seems to have been favoured as the place of burial of people of property; death is no less a sphere for competition than life. The area had great ritual importance of the area: the procession of the initiates to the Eleusinian Mysteries left the city for Eleusis through the Kerameikos by way of the Sacred Gate, while the Panathenaic procession marshalled at the Dipylon Gate before passing through the Agora toward the

Figure 8.11 Remains of the Kerameikos.

Acropolis. All of this made the Kerameikos a natural place for elite burials.

It was probably for the same reason that the Kerameikos was selected as the location for state burials. Particularly important were the communal burials of the war dead in the state burial ground (*Demosion Sema*). The Athenians were unusual in the way they treated their war dead. The general custom in ancient Greece was to bury the dead on the field of battle, but the Athenians burned their dead where they fell and brought the remains home. They then held a state funeral at the end of each war year for those who had died in battle for the city. Our principal ancient source for the practice is Thucydides in his introduction to the funeral speech pronounced by Perikles over the Athenian dead at the end of the first year of the Peloponnesian War:[18]

> In the same winter the Athenians according to their ancestral custom gave a funeral at public expense to those who had first fallen in this war in the following way. Three days beforehand they erect a tent and lay out the bones of the dead; and each person brings to their relatives any offerings they please. When the funeral procession takes place, cypress coffins are carried on wagons, one for each tribe; the bones of the deceased are placed in the coffin of their tribe. One empty bier is carried decked for the missing, that is, for those who could not be found for burial. Any citizen or stranger who wishes joins in the funeral: and the female relatives are there wailing at the burial. They put them in the public memorial [*demosion sema*] in the most beautiful suburb of the city [i.e. the Kerameikos], in which they always bury those who fall in war; with the exception of those slain at Marathon, whom they placed in a tomb on the spot because they judged their valour extraordinary. After they cover the bodies with earth, a man chosen by the polis, who is considered intelligent and of outstanding reputation, pronounces over them a fitting praise; after which they all disperse. This is how they bury them.

Thucydides describes an event which combines public and private, family and state ceremony, but which in its outlines is essentially a remodelling of the normal family funeral at civic level. We do not know how far back this particular practice goes, yet its antecedents are very illustrious. Before the age of oratory, lyric poetry was the medium for ornate celebration of the dead, and we have evidence for the commissioning of distinguished lyric poets to produce laments in praise of aristocrats and rulers. The Athenian funeral oration appropriates the role previously played by such laments and places those who die for the democratic polis on the same level as the aristocratic dead of former generations. The content of the funeral oration, which praises not just the dead but the traditions, the political system and the culture which produced them, made the event a celebration of the whole polis, a reaffirmation of the collective identity of the inhabitants and a source of pride both for the citizen and the non-citizen population. The dead were also celebrated on these occasions with funeral games. These are attested in the literary sources, while the evidence of archaeology seems to point to horse races in the Kerameikos. The antecedents of these funeral games are again aristocratic and go back to Homer. Like the funeral speech, the effect is to turn the ordinary citizens who die for the polis into an elite.

The dead were buried together and their names recorded on ten lists, one per tribe, each of which simply gave the name, without family details, in contrast to private memorials. It is the relationship with the polis that counts. The dead from different campaigns were not buried all in a single enclosure. The Demosion Sema was an area, not a single tomb. Collectively, the public tombs must have been very impressive; the location of the war memorials close to each other will have underlined and even stimulated the rhetoric of the funeral orations, which tended to place the deeds of the newly dead in the context of past triumphs. Excavations north-west of the current Kerameikos archaeological site have revealed a number of mass burials. The physical condition of the dead (based on the bones) point to men in their prime, while the pottery finds date the sites securely to the fifth century. These appear, therefore, to be casualties from the Peloponnesian War; they may even include the remains over which Perikles delivered his funeral speech. Archaeological evidence suggests that these collective burials continued into the third century.

The public monuments must always have dominated the area, but they will have been all the more impressive during the fifth century, because the monumental quality of the Kerameikos area as a whole was muted. Athenian funerary monuments became very austere from the late sixth to the latter part of the fifth century. It has been suggested plausibly that this absence of elaborate private tombs is to be linked to the custom of public burial of the war dead; the state appropriated the war dead and with them the exclusive right to impressive monuments. It is difficult to determine, however, whether this is a matter of law or just a shared reluctance to compete with the collective memorialization. Cicero speaks of a law banning lavish monuments:[19]

> But sometime after [i.e. after Solon] because of these sumptuous tombs, which we see in the Ceramicus, it was enshrined in law that

Figure 8.12 Graves in the Kerameikos, including the cenotaph of Dexileos, killed in battle in 394.

> 'nobody is to make a tomb which requires more labour than ten men can achieve in three days'.

but the chronology is too vague to be of much help. Private tombs become more substantial in the second half of the fifth century and sculpture reappears in the last quarter of the century; by the early fourth century, we find impressive private cenotaphs for those killed in war, whose remains will still have been buried in the Demosion Sema. Evidently an accommodation has been found between the claims of the state and the claims of the elite families.

9

Democracy and Its Critics

The past is never transparent; and it is never inert, unless it is very remote indeed. It is endlessly rewritten in the light of contemporary need and experience and constantly cited for its capacity to influence thinking in the present. The evaluation of Athenian democracy has been particularly prone to fluctuation according to the constitutional context of the researcher. For most readers in the western world at the beginning of the twenty-first century, the superiority of democracy over other systems is an uncontested fact. But for eighteenth-century writers 'democracy' was not a positive term, and this attitude spilled over into the nineteenth. In a much-quoted statement, the poet Wordsworth observed: 'I am of that odious class of men called democrats.' It was not until the latter part of the nineteenth century that democracy became (in the language of *1066 and All That*) an incontestably Good Thing.

But Athenian democracy was controversial even for its contemporaries. In classical Greece the dominant form of government was aristocracy. Though Athens was far from being the only democracy and was probably not the first, it was unusual in maintaining democracy almost uninterrupted for the best part of two centuries. Our surviving texts from the period all come from members of the elite, and not surprisingly some are highly critical of democracy.

For some critics, the root problem with democracy is the notion of equality. Though the Athenians never adopted the view that all members of society are equal in terms of ability, at heart democracy assumes that collective decisions are more reliable than individual decisions and that all people are, to some degree, capable of intelligent thought. There is, in fact, modern research which suggests that in certain circumstances a large group is more likely to reach the right decision that an individual. But an Assembly made up of artisans, labourers and traders inevitably aroused a degree of disdain in anyone convinced of the natural right of the aristocrat to rule; this disdain finds expression in the dismissive remarks of Xenophon's Sokrates on the membership of the Athenian Assembly.[1] The principle of *isegoria*, equal voice, goes further, since equal access to the rostrum presupposes that the advice of the poor can be as useful as that of the rich and the layman's advice as good as the dedicated politician. Plato's Sokrates pokes mischievous fun at the principle that anyone should address the Assembly:[2]

> I observe that whenever we gather in the Assembly, when the city must deal with building they send for builders to advise on the buildings, and when it's about the construction of ships, we send for the shipbuilders, and this is the case with everything else which they think can be learned and taught. And if anyone else whom they don't consider a craftsman tries to advise them, even if he's handsome or rich or one of the noble, they still don't tolerate it but laugh and heckle, until the man attempting to speak is forced by the din to step down or the archers drag or carry him off on the orders of the Prytaneis. This is how they act on issues which they think are a matter of skill. But when there is need for a decision on the running of the city, a carpenter will stand up and advise them, a smith or cobbler – it's all the same – a trader or ship's captain, rich or poor, highborn or low, and nobody opposes these as in the cases mentioned before, because, though he has not learned from any source and he has no teacher, he still attempts to offer advice.

The Theban herald in Euripides' *Suppliant Women* is equally dismissive:[3]

> The poor farmer,
> even if he were not ignorant, because of his work
> could not turn his gaze to public affairs.
> This causes vexation for the better men
> when some low man [*poneros*] has prestige
> winning over the *demos* with his tongue, when he was nothing before.

The same prejudice is expressed by the Old Oligarch, who observes that the advantage for the masses is that the speakers have the same (low) aims as themselves and therefore operate to their common advantage.[4] Aristotle is critical of egalitarianism based on number rather than merit.[5] One of the speakers in Herodotos' fictitious debate on constitutional models observes that the mass is uneducated and unintelligent.[6] Ultimately what we have here is simple class prejudice based on the traditional claim to superiority of those with old money. This was a prejudice daily reinforced by the survival of a vocabulary which identified social status with moral superiority: the wealthy were 'the best men', *hoi aristoi*, 'the best element', *to beltiston*, while the word *poneros* could be used to mean 'rogue', 'villain' or by aristocratic writers to designate a man of low socio-economic status. This disdain for the mass was secretly shared by some politicians who achieved eminence under the democracy, to judge by Alkibiades' dismissal of democracy as 'acknowledged folly' in his speech at Sparta in Thucydides (though he is of course trying to win over a Spartan audience).[7]

Perhaps the best contemporary answer to these prejudices is offered by Thrasyboulos in the speech attributed to him by Xenophon in his account of the restoration of the democracy in 404:[8]

> 'My advice to you,' he said, 'men of the city [that is, those who had supported the Thirty, as distinct from the democrats who had seized Piraeius] is to know yourselves. The best way to do this is if you were to reflect why you should feel proud and seek to rule us. Is it because you are more just? But the demos, though more poor than you, has never yet done you wrong for money. But you, who are richer than everyone, have committed many shameful acts for profit. But since you have no claim to justice, ask yourselves if you should be proud of your courage. And what better test of this could there be than the way we warred against each other. But perhaps you could claim that you are superior in judgment; yet despite having city walls and heavy armour and the Peloponnesians for your allies you were deprived by men who had none of these advantages. Or do you think you should be proud

because of the Spartans? Why should you, when like men who muzzle and hand over biting dogs they have gone off, handing you over to the *demos* here that you have wronged.'

Critics also associate democracy with indiscipline. The freedom (*eleutheria*) on which the Athenians prided themselves is for Plato the root cause of the destruction of democracy.[9] In his view, it degenerates into total indiscipline, though the democratic society he depicts (in which fathers fear children, teachers fear pupils, and the laws are held in contempt) is a grotesque parody of democratic Athens. The indiscipline at the heart of democracy is also emphasized by the Old Oligarch:[10]

> Throughout the world the best element [*to beltiston*] is hostile to democracy. For among the best there is least indiscipline and injustice and the most scrupulous commitment to good conduct, while in the *demos* there is the most disorder and lack of scruple [*poneria*].

Though rich in irony, in view of the contempt of the Athenian oligarchs for law and morality, this is a view shared by other critics of democracy. It is found in Isokrates' complaint that the Athenian constitution in his day (the first half of the fourth century) confused lawlessness (*paranomia*) with freedom (*eleutheria*).[11] The idea is already present in Herodotos' debate on the constitutions, where the unruly passion of the mob is compared by one speaker to a winter torrent.[12] It occurs again in Herodotos' own throwaway remark about the ease with which Aristagoras, the fomenter of the Ionian revolt in the 490s, persuaded the Athenians to back him after failing dismally to enlist the help of the Spartan king Kleomenes: 'it seems that it is easier to deceive many than one.'[13] The same idea lurks behind Thucydides' criticism of the Athenians for fickleness in first deposing and fining and then reinstating Perikles as general early in the Peloponnesian War.[14] For Plato, this lack of discipline is particularly manifested in the conduct of the Assembly and the courts, where instead of listening in disciplined silence the crowds interrupt noisily. This notion is already present in Pindar's dismissal of the demos as *ho labros stratos*, 'the raucous crowd'.[15] It is picked up in republican Rome by Cicero:[16]

> And so, to leave aside the present Greece which has long been battered and afflicted by its own bad judgment, that Greece of old, which once flourished in wealth, power and renown, fell because of this one thing, the immoderate freedom (*libertas*) and indiscipline (*licentia*) of its assemblies.

But again there is little in the contemporary criticism beyond the disgruntlement of the aristocrat at the lack of an exclusive right to power, and the absence of a culture of automatic deference to status and authority. The Assembly could lose its head, and the Athenians knew it, as they showed when they reopened the debate on Mytilene in 427 after voting to massacre the grown men and enslave the rest of the population. But we have seen that Assembly meetings, though lively, were orderly – remarkably so, given their scale. It is important to bear in mind that the critics of democracy will rarely if ever have witnessed a political debate in a non-democratic state; they are comparing the Athenian reality with an abstract ideal, an error repeated by many moderns. Thucydides' account of the debate at Sparta which led to the Peloponnesian War is proof that fierce debate was a feature of Greek, not just democratic, politics.[17]

Plato sees democracy as a constitution which breeds not just unruly but also violent passions. But speakers addressing the Assembly or court are as prone to criticize the Athenians for being too soft-hearted. Since the context is often an argument for severity, we cannot be too trusting. But the picture is reproduced in *Athenian Constitution*. Of the expulsion of the tyrants, the author notes:[18] 'The Athenians allowed all the friends of the tyrants who were not implicated in wrongdoing during the disturbances to live in the city, with the usual leniency of the *demos*.' The demos showed the same generosity after the Thirty in declaring an amnesty. Plato notes in his *Seventh Letter* that the returning democrats behaved with great 'decency'/'moderation' (*epieikeia*), while the *Athenian Constitution*, commenting on the amnesty and the decision of the democrats to repay as the city's debt the money the Thirty had borrowed from Sparta to sustain their regime, observes:[19] 'I think that of all men they responded to the preceding disasters in the most honourable and public-spirited (*politikotata*) manner, both individually and collectively.'

More serious is the accusation that the Assembly was too easily swayed by skilful speakers. It is here that Thucydides locates the flaws in post-Periklean democracy. For Thucydides, democracy required strong leaders; the masses needed to be restrained and the great strength of Perikles was his ability to control the Assembly through his remarkable personal authority. Perikles' successors were all competing on an equal footing and in their struggle for dominance were inclined to give the masses their own way.[20] There is much that is inaccurate in all of this. It is important to note that some ancient commentators made not Kleon but Perikles the first of the demagogues and attributed some at least of his democratic measures as an attempt to curry favour with the demos; the narrative of decline and fall could be written in more than one way. The picture of Perikles' successors as motivated solely by ambition is heavily influenced by Thucydides' own disappointment at the way in which (as he saw it) the successes of the decades of expansion were squandered.

But Thucydides is not alone in arguing that the democratic Assembly is too easily seduced by a clever speaker. This danger is identified by the Theban herald in Euripides' *Suppliant Women* and again by the messenger in Euripides' *Orestes*. Though the former is an unsympathetic figure, the latter is more difficult to dismiss and it seems that the Athenians themselves identified this as a risk attached to collective decision-making. The danger is inevitable wherever policy is shaped by open debate rather than by fiat or by cabal, though experience also shows that the absence of such debate does not so much prevent haste and error as facilitate its concealment. The Athenian answer was to make the public speaker answerable for his proposals. Of course, the demos was not answerable for its response, and speakers occasionally comment on the fact that the speakers are held responsible for collective decisions.[21] The complaint has some force. But those voting at the Assembly did not escape scot-free, since collectively they felt the impact of policy errors and in military matters could pay with their lives.

Modern critics of Athenian democracy have often echoed the hostility of Athenian writers to the radical democracy, and not surprisingly, since academics themselves have traditionally come from, or else joined, the modern elite. But there is another, and opposing strand, which emphasizes the lack, not the excess, of democracy in Athens. Athens never extended political rights to women, resident aliens or slaves. This was explicitly and irrevocably a democracy of adult Athenian males. But it is important to bear in mind that the granting of political rights to women is a very recent phenomenon, for most societies a product of the twentieth (in some the twenty-first) century. In Britain at least women owed their political rights as much to world war as to enlightened policy. The exclusion of foreigners from political rights is the norm in modern systems, which differ only in their greater readiness to allow outsiders to acquire citizenship. It is probably the exclusion of slaves, as possessions, from almost all rights which particularly offends the modern reader, though for most of the Founding Fathers of the United States it was perfectly compatible with democracy. One cannot avoid the sheer brutality of chattel slavery and ancient justifications of slavery, even when argued with the acumen of an Aristotle,[22] make uncomfortable reading, even more so when they recur in the mouths of defenders of slavery in antebellum America. But Athens was no better and no worse than any other Greek state of its day, and most subsequent states until the nineteenth century. The defects of the Athenian system, measured against modern ideals, are too obvious to ignore; but compared with most subsequent political systems, Athens was remarkably egalitarian.

Another factor which has suggested a democratic deficit in Athens is the role of the elite. The players on the political field were almost always wealthy men and the majority acted as referees, not strikers. Here is Demosthenes' memorable account of the Assembly meeting after Philip's seizure of Elateia in 338:[23]

> Next day at dawn the Prytaneis called the Council to the Council chamber and you made your way to the Assembly, and before the Council had completed its business and drafted its proposals, the

> whole people was seated up on the hill. Then when the Council had arrived and the Prytaneis had announced the news they had received and brought up the messenger and he had spoken, the herald asked: 'who wishes to speak?' Nobody came forward. Though he repeated the question many times, still nobody stood up . . .

Demosthenes is describing an emergency so startling that the regular speakers are silent. But in one respect the meeting was typical, in that most ordinary Athenians would never address the Assembly; their response to the herald's invitation was always to remain in their seats. The elite changed in composition during the classical period, with wealth replacing a combination of wealth and birth as the qualification for membership. But, whatever its composition, there was always an elite. In this respect again Athens was not unusual. It is difficult to identify a contemporary developed society which does not have an elite. The Athenians were pragmatic enough to accept this. Their aim was not to remove the elite but to ensure that the last word in policy went to the demos and that politicians were always subject to popular scrutiny and control.

Finally, many moderns have questioned the accuracy of the democratic mantra 'live as one pleases', and more generally whether the Athenians had any conception of individual rights. Certainly the terminology is lacking. The Athenians had a term for positive political rights, though the language used was of 'privilege'/'honour' (*time*) rather than 'right'. But they had no term for individual 'rights' in the modern sense. However, the broader term of *eleutheria* included non-interference by the polis in individual activity which neither threatened the polis nor harmed others. The system did, of course, produce abuses. Although its fatal outcome was more the result of his intransigence than any fundamental flaw in the legal system, it is almost certain that Sokrates' conviction was motivated by residual resentment against the Thirty. The execution of Sokrates was at least the result of due legal process. But law could be brushed aside in extreme circumstances, as when the generals were tried all together after Arginousai in contravention of a basic legal principle. But these are exceptions; and there is scarcely a democracy in existence where the same tale could not be told.

Ultimately the test of a constitution must be its success in serving the needs of its population. For virtually two centuries Athens enjoyed almost uninterrupted internal stability. Political rivalry, though fierce and not infrequently devastating for politicians and generals, was conducted through constitutional means and according to law. Tension between rich and poor was contained. The rich were compelled to contribute to the state, but there was never (under the democracy) any attempt to strip them of their wealth. Though a wide gulf separated the rich from the poor, attempts were made to protect the most vulnerable members of society. From a utilitarian perspective (the greatest good for the greatest number of people), the Athenian constitution could be judged a success.

During the same period Athens was one of the foremost powers in Greece. For most of the fifth century Athens was the largest and wealthiest, and arguably the most powerful, state on the peninsula. Stripped of empire, walls and ships at the end of the fifth century and reduced to the role of a Spartan vassal, it had recovered sufficient strength within a decade to play a major role in Greek politics, which it did for most of the fourth century. The picture is of course not one of undiluted success. Athens lost the Peloponnesian War and with hindsight one can see mistakes which could have been avoided. But the defeat was as much the result of Spartan access to Persian gold as of Athenian errors. Athens won and lost an empire; but the Spartan supremacy which followed was much shorter (it lasted only two decades) and far more oppressive. Ultimately Athens was no match for Macedon, with its vast mineral wealth, its concentration of power in the person of the king, and (crucially) the succession of two quite remarkable rulers, Philip and Alexander. Nor was any other Greek state, irrespective of its constitution.

There is, of course, more to success than power. During the lifetime of the democracy, Athens set the cultural agenda for Greece. In the fifth century, though many of the leading intellectuals were of non-Athenian origin, and though they travelled widely in Greece, it was Athens in particular where they found an environment congenial to their activity. The move from physical speculation to ethics as the essence of philosophy (an agenda which has survived to the present day) took place at Athens. Historiography, though originating in Ionia, became quintessentially Athenian. The successor to Herodotos of Halikarnassos was the Athenian Thucydides. Though Greek prose originated primarily in Ionia, by the end of the fifth century Attic Greek had become the language of prose-writing. Hence Gorgias of Leontinoi in Sicily chooses to write in Attic Greek, not in Ionian or in his native dialect. Perikles' vision of Athens as the school of Hellas is reflected in the export of Athenian tragedy to other parts of Greece, from Aischylos in Sicily early in the fifth century to Euripides and Agathon in Macedonia at the end. In the fourth century (some would argue earlier) Athenian comedy becomes international, and Athens attracts both tragic and comic writers from other parts of Greece.

Notes

1 First Thoughts

1 Pindar *P.*2.87–8.
2 Herodotos 4.137.2, 6.43.3, 131.1, Aristophanes *Acharnians* 642.
3 *Suppliants* 604.
4 *Politics* 1291b–92a, 1318b–19a.
5 Herodotos 6.131.1, Thucydides 2.37.1, 3.37, Aischines e.g. 1.5–6, Demosthenes e.g. 21.207.
6 Thucydides 1.22.1.
7 *Aristeides* 7.5–6.
8 Plato, *Protagoras* 318e–319a.

2 The Road to Democracy

1 *Athenian Constitution* 3.6, 8.2.
2 *Athenian Constitution* 2.2.
3 *Athenian Constitution* 3.4.
4 Thucydides 1.126.8.
5 Thucydides 1. 1.126–7, Herodotos 5.71.
6 *Athenian Constitution* 4.1.
7 Plutarch *Solon* 15.2.
8 Solon fr.36W.8ff.
9 Fr.36W.5ff.
10 *Athenian Constitution* 2.3.
11 *Athenian Constitution* 2.2.
12 *Athenian Constitution* 7.1.
13 *Athenian Constitution* 9.1.
14 *Athenian Constitution* 26.2.
15 *Athenian Constitution* 8.4, Plutarch *Solon* 19.1.
16 *Athenian Constitution* 8.4.
17 *Athenian Constitution* 13.1.

18 *Athenian Constitution* 13, Plutarch *Solon* 2.9.1, Herodotos 1.59.3.

19 *Athenian Constitution* 14–15, Herodotos 1.59–64.

20 Thucydides 6.54.5–6.

21 *Athenian Constitution* 16.5.

22 *Athenian Constitution* 16.2.

23 Herodotos 5.66, *Athenian Constitution* 20.1.

24 Herodotos 5.65.1.

25 *Athenian Constitution* 21.1.

26 *Athenian Constitution* 21.4, Aristotle *Politics* 1275b34–7.

27 *IG* i[3] 105.

28 *Athenian Constitution* 22.2.

29 *Athenian Constitution* 20.3, Herodotos 5.69–76.

30 Herodotos 6.102, 107–09.

31 *Athenian Constitution* 22.5.

32 *Athenian Constitution* 25, 27.1, Plutarch *Kimon* 15.2.

33 Aristotle *Politics*1304a17ff., *Athenian Constitution* 23.1.

34 *Athenian Constitution* 25.2.

35 Herodotos 6.136.2–3.

36 Thucydides 1.107.4.

37 *Athenian Constitution* 26.2.

38 Thucydides 2.65.10.

39 For the *choregos*, see 3.3 below.

40 *Acharnians* 380–81, *Wasps* 1034.

41 *Athenian Constitution* 28.3.

42 Aischines 2.76.

43 Lysias 30.13.

44 Thucydides 6.53.3, 6.60.1.

45 Thucydides 8.65.3, *Athenian Constitution* 29.5.

46 8.97.2.

47 *Athenian Constitution* 35.2.

48 Aristophanes *Frogs* 688–91.

49 *Athenian Constitution* 39.6.

50 Aischines 3.38, Demosthenes 20.89, 93, 24.18, 33.

51 41.2.

52 *Athenian Constitution* 41.3.

53 *Athenian Constitution* 49.3.

54 Andokides 1.84.
55 [Demosthenes]59.80.
56 Harding no. 78, Rhodes-Osborne no. 58.
57 Deinarchos 1.1, 1.50.
58 Deinarchos 1.54.
59 Harding no. 101, Rhodes-Osborne no. 79.
60 Deinarchos 1.62.
61 *Athenian Constitution* 7.4.
62 *Athenian Constitution* 47.1.

3 Democracy and Ideology

1 *Athenian Constitution* 62.3.
2 Aristotle *Politics* 1322b37–23a7, 1319b28–33.
3 Isokrates 7.37, 46, *Athenian Constitution* 3.6.
4 *Knights* 578–80.
5 Lysias 16.18–19.
6 Plutarch *Perikles* 32.2.
7 3.62.4.
8 Xenophon *Memorabilia* 1.2.35–6, *Athenian Constitution* 4.3, 30.2, 31.1, 63.3.
9 Thucydides 2.37.1.
10 *Athenian Constitution* 56.2.
11 Demosthenes 20.108.
12 *Athenian Constitution* 26.4, 42.1, Plutarch *Perikles* 37.3.
13 Aristophanes *Birds* 1649–52.
14 [Demosthenes]59.16.
15 *Athenian Constitution* 42.1.
16 Aristophanes *Frogs* 31–4, 693–4, Hellanikos fr.171, Diodoros 13.97.1.
17 Meiggs-Lewis no.85; cf. Lysias 13.70–73.
18 Demosthenes 45.85.
19 [Demosthenes]59.89–91, cf. *IG* ii^2 103.
20 [Demosthenes]59.92.
21 Lysias 24.13, 27, *Athenian Constitution* 49.4.
22 E.g. Thucydides 2.46, Aristotle *Politics* 1268a8–11, *Athenian Constitution* 24.3.

23 Harding 8A.
24 Thucydides 6.42.
25 *Athenian Constitution* 42.3.
26 *Athenian Constitution* 53.2–5.
27 Lysias 6.24, Aischines 3.176.
28 Aischines 1.29.

4 The Core Bodies

1 *Athenian Constitution* 43.2.
2 For Kleon see Aristophanes *Knights* 774–6, for Demosthenes e.g. Demosthenes 19.154, Aischines 2.17.
3 *Athenian Constitution* 43.2.
4 Xenophon *Memorabilia* 1.1.18, Lysias 31.1, [Demosthenes]59.4.
5 *Athenian Constitution* 62.2.
6 *Athenian Constitution* 43.3.
7 Aristophanes *Assemblywomen* 442–4, Lysias 31.31, Aischines 3.125.
8 *Athenian Constitution* 62.2.
9 *Athenian Constitution* 44.1.
10 Demosthenes 18.169.
11 *Athenian Constitution* 45.4.
12 Aischines 2.58.
13 Aischines 2.45–6.
14 *Athenian Constitution* 47.1, 49.5.
15 *Athenian Constitution* 47.2.
16 Andokides 1.133–6, [Demosthenes]59.27, *Athenian Constitution* 47.2, Harpocration under *metoikion*, Aischines 1.119.
17 *Athenian Constitution* 47. For the King-Archon, see section 5.2 below.
18 *Athenian Constitution* 47.2, 3.
19 *Athenian Constitution* 47.3, 48.1.
20 Meiggs-Lewis no. 46.
21 *Athenian Constitution* 48.3–4.
22 *Athenian Constitution* 49.3, 46.2.
23 *Athenian Constitution* 46.1, Demosthenes 22.8.
24 *Athenian Constitution* 45.2.

25 Lysias 13.21–3, Demosthenes 24.63, 144–6.

26 Aischines 1.112.

27 *Athenian Constitution* 49.1.

28 Lysias 16.6–7, Harpocration entry under *katastasis.*

29 *Athenian* 49.4.

30 *Athenian Constitution* 45.3.

31 *Athenian Constitution* 42.2

32 Xenophon *Memorabilia* 1.2.42, Eupolis *Baptai* fr.76KA.

33 Demosthenes 20.89, 93–4, 24.18–23, 33 Aischines 3.38–40.

34 Thucydides 2.22.1.

35 See 4.1 above.

36 Aischines 2.15.

37 Thucydides 8.72.2.

38 Thucydides 8.67.2.

39 *Athenian Constitution* 41.3.

40 *Athenian Constitution* 62.2.

41 *Athenian Constitution* 44.2.

42 Aristophanes *Acharnian* 54, Plato *Protagoras* 319c.

43 *Assemblywomen* 20–1, *Acharnians* (line 4).

44 Prayer Deinarchos 2.14, Aischin.1.23, curse Deinarchos 2.16, Demosthenes 19.70, Aristophanes' parody *Women at the Thesmophoria* (352–71).

45 *IG* ii^3 1 900, 4–8, Theophrastos *Characters* 21.11; the role of divination in public affairs is discussed further at pp. 101–4.

46 Aischines 3.4.

47 Thucydides 4.27.5–28.3.

48 Plato *Republic* 492b–c.

49 Meiggs-Lewis no 85.

50 See on this pp. 75, 77, 97.

51 *Athenian Constitution* 41.2.

52 *Athenian Constitution* 9.1.

53 Demosthenes 54.39.

54 Aristophanes *Knights* 50–1, 800.

55 *Athenian Constitution* 27.4.

56 *Wasps* 242–4, 303–5.

57 *Athenian Constitution* 27.5.

58 Aristophanes *Assemblywomen* 681–90, *Athenian Constitution* 63–5.

59 Andokides 1.17.

60 *Athenian Constitution* 55.2.

61 *Athenian Constitution* 48.4–5, 54.2, Aischines 3.23.

62 For the nomothetai, see 2.11, 4.2 above.

63 Plutarch *Perikles* 32.1, Diodoros 12.39.2, Athenaios 589[e]; for impiety trials, see further pp. 104–6.

5 Serving the Democracy

1 Herodotos 3.131.2, Aristophanes *Acharnians* 1030, *IG* 1[3] 164.

2 Aristophanes *Frogs* 1084.

3 *Athenian Constitution* 24.3.

4 *Agoranomoi Athenian Constitution* 51.1, *metronomoi* 51.2, *sitophylakes*, 51.3, *emporiou epimeletai* 51.4.

5 *Athenian Constitution* 50.2–3.

6 *Athenian Constitution* 54.1.

7 *Eisagogeis Athenian Constitution* 51.2, the Forty 53.1–3, the Eleven 52.1.

8 *Athenian Constitution* 47.2; cf. 4.1 above.

9 Meiggs-Lewis no 79.

10 *Athenian Constitution* 48.1–2, 54.2.

11 *Athenian Constitution* 54.6–7.

12 *Athenian Constitution* 62.2.

13 *Athenian Constitution* 59.1–6.

14 Eponymous Archon (usually called just 'the Archon') *Athenian Constitution* 56.3–7, King-Archon *Athenian Constitution* 57, Polemarchos *Athenian Constitution* 58.

15 *Athenian Constitution* 56.1.

16 24.112.

17 Xenophon *Memorabilia* 1.2.9, Aristotle *Rhetoric* 1393b3ff.

18 *Athenian Constitution* 43.1, 61.

19 *Athenian Constitution* 43.1.

20 *Athenian Constitution* 43.1.

21 Aischines 3.25, Demosthenes 3.29. For the theoric fund, see also 3.3 above.

22 *Athenian Constitution* 43.1.

23 *Athenian Constitution* 47.2.

24 [Plutarch], *Lives of the Ten Orators* 852b, Diodoros Siculus 16.88.1.

25 Hypereides fr.118.

26 'Prytany secretary' *Athenian Constitution* 54.3, Council 'law secretary' 54.4, secretary of the Thesmothetai 55.1, secretary to the Council and the Assembly 54.5.

27 *Athenian Constitution* 47.5, Dem.19.129.

28 Antiphon 1.20, Aischin.2.126.

29 Lysias 30.29.

30 [Demosthenes]58.8.

31 *Frogs* 1084, Demosthenes19.70.

32 Noted by Aristotle, *Politics* 1305a11ff.

33 Aristophanes *Peace* 679–81.

34 Thucydides 8.68.1.

35 *Peace* 1032–4.

36 Deinarchos 1.71.

37 *Athenian Constitution* 4.2.

38 Thucydides 3.43.4.

39 Thucydides 1.126; for Kylon see 2.1 above.

40 Thucydides 6.16.2.

41 [Demosthenes]59.43.

42 Perikles *Athenian Constitution* 27.1, Hyperbolos Aristophanes *Acharnians* 845–7.

43 Antiphon 5.69–70.

44 Thucydides 2.65.3–4.

45 Thucydides 4.55.3.

46 Xenophon *Hellenica* 1.7.1–34.

47 Deinarchos 1.14, 3.17.

48 Aischines 2.107.

49 Demosthenes 19.277–9.

50 Diodoros 15.35.

51 *Aristeides* 7.7.

52 *Aristeides* 7.5, *Alkibiades* 13, *Nikias* 11.

53 *Athenian Constitution* 43.5.

54 Thucydides 8.73.3.

55 Hypereides 4.7–8.

56 For *graphe paranomon*, see 4.3 above.

57 Aischines 3.194.
58 Hypereides 4.8.
59 Hypereides 5.24–5.

6 Religion in the Democratic City

1 Cf. Aischines 1.23.
2 Thuc. 2.24.1.
3 *IG* i[3], 1330, translation by Lambert and Osborne.
4 Aischines 3.18.
5 *Birds* 716–22.
6 Speech 4, *For Euxenippos*.
7 Herodotos 7.141–3.
8 *Birds* 1958–91.
9 Thuc.8.1.1.
10 *IG* ii[2] 17.
11 See pp. 76–7.
12 Thuc.6.27–8.
13 Thuc.1.38.1.
14 *Acharnians* 252–63.
15 The locations mentioned here are discussed further in Chapter 8.
16 Demosthenes 21.103, 39.16, 22.68.
17 See p. 48.
18 *Athenian Constitution* 3.5, [Dem.]59.73.
19 Demosthenes 57.46.
20 Demosthenes 5 (*On the peace*) was delivered during the heated debate.

7 Local Government: The Demes

1 Demosthenes 57.10.
2 Plutarch *Perikles* 37.3, Aristophanes *Wasps* 716–18, Demosthenes 57, Aischines 1.77, 86.
3 For the public arbitrator, see 3.3 above.
4 *Athenian Constitution* 62.1.

5 Demosthenes 57.25–6.
6 See p. 111.
7 Isaios 3.80.
8 Demosthenes 57.63.
9 [Demosthenes]43.57–8.
10 *Athenian Constitution* 42.1.
11 Demosthenes 57.26.

8 The Democratic Landscape

1 Thucydides 6.54.6.
2 *Knights* 153, 156.
3 Xenophon *Hellenica* 2.3.50–6.
4 Aristophanes *Peace* 1181–4.
5 For the *poletai*, see pp. 60 and 81.
6 See p. 62.
7 Plutarch *Themistokles* 19.4.
8 Aischines 2.61, Dem.21.8.
9 For the *ephebeia*, see Chapter 3, p. 53.
10 *Athenian Constitution* 42.4; for the *ephebeia*, see 3.3 above.
11 *Knights* 42.
12 Aristophanes *Lysistrata* 912–13 (742–55).
13 Aischines 2.74, 2.105.
14 See 3.3 above.
15 Isokrates 8.82.
16 Aischines 3.154.
17 [Xenophon] *Athenian Constitution* 2.18.
18 Thucydides 2.34.
19 *De legibus* 2.26.65.

9 Democracy and Its Critics

1 *Memorabilia* 3.7.5–6.
2 Plato *Protagoras* 319c–d.

3 Euripides *Suppliant Women* 420–5.
4 [Xenophon] *Athenian Constitution* 1.6.
5 *Politics* 1301a29–40.
6 Herodotos 3.81.2.
7 Thucydides 6.89.6.
8 Xenophon *Hellenica* 2.4.40–41.
9 *Republic* 562–3.
10 [Xenophon] *Athenian Constitution* 1.5.
11 Isokrates 7.20.
12 Herodotos 3.81.2.
13 Herodotos 5.97.2.
14 Thucydides 2.65.3–4
15 Pindar *Pythian* 2.87.
16 *Pro Flacco* 16.
17 Thucydides 1.79–86.
18 *Athenian Constitution* 22.4.
19 *Athenian Constitution* 40.2.
20 Thucydides 2.65.10.
21 Thucydides 2.60.4, 3.43.4.
22 *Politics* 1254b.
23 Demosthenes 18.169–70.

Appendix 1

Suggested Further Reading

The volume of material on the subject is enormous and all I can do here is to flag some of the more important contributions.

Sources

All classical texts quoted are translated by me unless otherwise indicated. Few of the literary sources require explanation. Solon is cited according to the numbering of the second edition of the large Oxford text of Martin West (*Iambi et elegi Graeci*). Fragments of the historians are cited according to the numbering of the magisterial multi-volume edition of Felix Jacoby, *Die Fragmente der griechischen Historischer* (Berlin/Leiden 1923–58), now available online from Brill in a collaborative revised edition under Ian Worthington, comic fragments according to the magnificent 8 volume *Poetae Comici Graeci* of Kassel and Austin (1983–2001). Wherever possible inscriptions are cited from R. Meiggs and D.M. Lewis, *A Selection of Greek Historical Inscriptions to the End of the Fifth Century* (Oxford 1969), P.J. Rhodes and R.G. Osborne, *Greek Historical Inscriptions, 404–323* BC (revised Oxford 2007), or from P. Harding, *From the End of the Peloponnesian War to the Battle of Ipsus* (Cambridge 1985), less frequently from the monumental *Inscriptiones Graecae* (Berlin 1873), also now available in part online. The general reader wishing to access the *Athenian Constitution* could not do better than to acquire the Penguin translation of P.J. Rhodes, *Aristotle: The Athenian Constitution* (Harmondsworth 1984). Rhodes also produced a weighty commentary, *A Commentary on the Aristotelian Athenaion Politeia* (Oxford 1981), which remains invaluable.

Luca Asmonti's *Athenian Democracy: A Sourcebook* (London, Bloomsbury 2015) offers a valuable collection of ancient sources.

General

The range of books which offer a historical setting for the study of Athenian democracy include:

S. Hornblower, *The Greek World 479–323*, 4th ed. (London 2011)
R. Sealey, *A History of the Greek City States 700–338 BC.* (Berkeley and Los Angeles 1976)
R. Brock and S Hodkinson, *Alternatives to Athens* (Oxford 2000)
P.J. Rhodes, *A History of the Classical Greek world: 478–323 BC*, 2nd ed. (London 2010)

The distribution of democratic regimes in Greece is examined in Eric Robinson, *Democracy Beyond Athens* (Cambridge 2011). J.K. Davies, *Democracy and Classical Greece* (2nd ed., Cambridge MA 1993) offers an illuminating and suggestive narrative, with copious (but deft) use of sources. W.G. Forrest, *The Emergence of Greek Democracy* (London 1966), traces its theme as far as the emergence of the radical democracy. Paul Cartledge, *Democracy: A Life* (Oxford 2016), examines Athenian democracy within a larger context from the archaic period to modern times.

M.H. Hansen, *The Athenian Democracy in the Age of Demosthenes* (2nd ed., Bristol 1999), focuses on the fourth-century democracy but also offers an account of the evolution of the system. C. Hignett, *A History of the Athenian Constitution* (Oxford 1952), despite its age, remains a thoughtful and provocative account of the political development of Athens to the end of the fifth century. A.H.M. Jones, *Athenian Democracy* (Oxford 1957), provides a general overview of the operation of the democracy which, despite its age, is still useful. R.K. Sinclair, *Democracy and Participation in Athens* (Cambridge 1988), provides a wide-ranging account of the operation of the democracy. D. Stockton, *The Classical Athenian Democracy* (Oxford 1990), combines an evolutionary account with a description of the operation in the fifth century. J. Shear, *Polis and Revolution: Responding to Oligarchy in Classical Athens* (Cambridge 2011), deals specifically with the oligarchic revolutions of the late fifth century and the restoration.

A number of edited collections approach the democracy from a variety of angles. See, for example: *Ritual, Finance, Politics: Athenian Democratic Accounts Presented to David Lewis* (Oxford 1994), edited by R.G. Osborne and S. Hornblower; *Performance Culture and Athenian Democracy* (Cambridge 1999), by R.G. Osborne and S. Goldhill; *Ancient Greek Democracy: Readings and Sources* (Oxford 2004), by E. Robinson; *The Origins of Democracy in Ancient Greece* (Berkeley, Los Angeles and London 2007), by K. Raaflaub *et al.*; and *Athens and Athenian Democracy* (Cambridge 2010), a collection of essays by R. Osborne.

Political bodies

The following studies will allow readers to explore specific bodies in the democracy in greater detail:

Assembly

M. H. Hansen, *The Athenian Assembly in the Age of Demosthenes* (Oxford 1987). Less easily acquired, but invaluable on many matters of detail, is his two-volume collection of published articles, *The Athenian Ecclesia* (Copenhagen 1983, 1989).

Council

P.J. Rhodes, *The Athenian Boule* (Oxford 1972).

Areiopagos

R.W. Wallace, *The Areiopagos Council to 307 BC.* (Baltimore and London 1989). This detailed study offers an alternative on many points to the account offered in this volume.

The courts

D.M. MacDowell, *The Law in Classical Athens* (London 1978), R.A. Bauman, *Political Trials in Ancient Greece* (London and New York 1990), S.C. Todd, *The Shape of Athenian Law* (Oxford 1993), E.M. Harris, *Democracy and the Rule of Law in Classical Athens* (Cambridge 2006).

The demes

R. Osborne, *Demos: The Discovery of Classical Attika* (Cambridge 1985), on aspects of the demography, sociology, economics and politics of the demes. Also D. Whitehead, *The Demes of Attika 508/7–c.259* BC (Princeton NJ 1986), the most thorough study available of the demes.

The phratries

S.D. Lambert, *The Phratries of Attica* (Michigan 1993).

Politicians and officials

B.S. Strauss, *Athens after the Peloponnesian War* (New York 1986), though focused specifically on the period after the Athenian defeat, has valuable insights on the operation of political groups. W.R. Connor, *The New Politicians of Fifth-Century Athens* (2nd ed., Princeton NJ 1971) is the classic discussion of the change in politics and politicians in the late fifth century. The degree and nature of the change has been contested and a closely argued case for the ultimate continuity in the leadership during the fifth century is offered by C. Mann in *Die Demagogen und das Volk: zur politischen Kommunikation im Athen des 5. Jahrhunderts v. Chr.* (Berlin 2007). J.T. Roberts, *Accountability in Athenian government* (Madison WI 1983), addresses the central principle of the accountability of officials and politicians.

Mass and elite

The role of the elite in democratic Athens is studied by J. Ober, *Mass and Elite in Democratic Athens* (Princeton NJ 1989), and J.K. Davies, *Wealth and the power of wealth in classical Athens* (New York 1981). J. Ober, *Democracy and Knowledge* (Princeton 2008), discusses the structures of the democracy and makes a persuasive case for the value of the participatory model as a means for the sharing and transfer of knowledge, and as a major factor in the success of Athens.

Citizenship

The obligations attached to citizenship form the subject of P. Liddell, *Civic Obligation and Individual Liberty in Ancient Athens* (Oxford 2007), and (from the opposite direction) M.R. Christ, *The Bad Citizen in Classical Athens* (Cambridge 2006). The *choregia* is given detailed discussion in P. Wilson, *The Athenian Institution of the Khoregia* (Cambridge 2000). The trierarchy is discussed in the larger context of running the navy in V. Gabrielson, *Financing the Athenian Fleet: Public Taxation and Social Relations* (Baltimore MD 2010).

The empire

R. Meiggs, *The Athenian Empire* (Oxford 1972), and P.J. Rhodes, *The Athenian Empire: Greece and Rome New Surveys in the Classics* 17 (Oxford 1985), both focus on the Athenian empire, the former in detail and at length, the latter in a brief treatment more accessible to the general reader. There is an edited collection of (reprinted) papers which address different aspects of the Athenian empire by Polly Low, *The Athenian Empire* (Edinburgh 2008), while J. Ma and N.Papazarkadas bring together a collection of new studies in *Interpreting the Athenian Empire* (London 2009).

The monuments

J.M. Camp, *The Athenian Agora* (London 1986), deals with the administrative heart of Athens. J. Travlos, *Pictorial Dictionary of Ancient Athens* (New York 1971), is a rich source of information and images. R.E. Wycherley, *The Stones of Athens* (Princeton NJ 1978), offers an excellent general introduction to the ancient city, organized by area. The rich materials found during the metro construction in Athens formed the subject of an exhibition subsequently published in a volume edited by L. Parlama and N.C. Stampolidis, *Athens: The City Beneath the City* (Athens 2000). The case for the location of the archaic Agora to the east of the Acropolis has been incremental and so is still fragmented in journals and brief mentions in larger volumes.

The following are recommended for anyone wishing to explore the issue in detail: G.S. Dontas, 'The true Aglaurion', *Hesperia* 52 (1983) 47–63; D. Harris-Cline, 'Archaic Athens and the topography of the Kylon affair', BSA 94 (1999) 309–320; N. Robertson, 'The city centre of archaic Athens', *Hesperia* 67 (1998) 283–302; G.C.R. Schmalz, 'The Athenian prytaneion discovered', *Hesperia* 75 (2006), 33–81.

For the Kerameikos, see U. Knigge, *Kerameikos* (Athens 1991), D. C. Kurtz and J. Boardman, *Greek Burial Customs* (London 1971), I. Morris, *Death-ritual and Social Structure in Classical Antiquity* (Cambridge 1992).

Ideology and criticism

M.H. Hansen, *Was Athens a Democracy? Popular Rule, Liberty and Equality in Ancient and Modern Political Thought* (Copenhagen 1989), condenses a wealth of material into a short space. J. Ober and C. Hedrick (eds), *Demokratia: A Conversation on Democracies, Ancient and Modern* (Princeton NJ 1996), assemble a wide-ranging collection of essays by a number of eminent writers; for reactions to Athenian democracy from the classical period to the twentieth century, see also J.T. Roberts, *Athens on Trial: The Antidemocratic Tradition in Western Thought* (Princeton NJ 1994), A.W. Saxonhouse, *Athenian Democracy: Modern Mythmakers and Ancient Theorists* (Notre Dame and London 1996), offers a survey in Chapter 1 of the myths woven around Athens by modern scholars.

Religion

J.M. Bremmer, *Greek Religion: Greece and Rome New Surveys in the Classics* 24 (Oxford 1994), provides a brief but valuable introduction. R. Parker, *Athenian Religion: A History* (Oxford 1996), and *Polytheism and Society at Athens* (Oxford 2005), offers detailed treatment of Athenian religion. S. Price, *Religions of the Ancient Greeks* (Cambridge 1999), J. Mikalson, *Ancient Greek Religion* (2nd ed., London 2010) and L.B. Zaidman and P. Schmidt Pantel, *Religion in the Ancient Greek City* (Cambridge 1993), offer broad accounts of Greek religion, the last with emphasis on religion in its civic context. Bauman (above) deals with politically motivated trials for impiety. A collection of essays on Greek religion by S.C. Humphreys, *The Strangeness of Gods* (Oxford 2004), includes a discussion of religion in the demes. Nancy Evans, *Civic Rites: Democracy and Religion in Ancient Athens* (Berkeley/Los Angeles/London 2010) offers an overview of the role of religion in democratic Athens and treatment of the high profile prosecutions.

Theatre

The political dimension of Athenian theatre has attracted renewed attention (and some lively exchanges) over the last few decades and interest shows no signs of waning. This forms the subject of valuable essays on tragedy and comedy by S. Goldhill and J. Henderson in the collection of essays assembled by J.J. Winkler & Froma Zeitlin (eds), *Nothing to Do with Dionysos?* (Princeton NJ 1990). Recent contributions include a collection of essays edited by D.M. Carter, *Why Athens? A Reappraisal of Tragic Politics* (Oxford 2011), and another edited by C.B.R. Pelling, *Greek Tragedy and the Historian* (Oxford 1997).

Appendix 2

Glossary

Agora — Area to the north of the Acropolis, which served as the administrative centre of the city and also as a market place. The term agora is also used for the meetings of the deme assemblies (contrast *Ekklesia*)

arche — 'office', a term used both for individual officials and for boards.

Archon — literally 'ruler', the term can refer to any official but usually (especially in the plural) designates a specific group of prestigious public officials elected by lot, comprising the *Archon*, the *Archon-Basileus*, the *Polemarchos* and the six *Thesmothetai*.

Archon-Basileus — 'King-Archon', one of the nine archons, with predominantly religious duties.

Areiopagos — in full 'the Council of the Areiopagos/Hill of Ares' (*he boule he ex Areiou Pagou*), named from its meeting place west of the Acropolis. The compendiary term Areiopagos, though convenient, is late; classical sources invariably use the full designation 'the Council of the Hill of Ares'.

atimia — literally 'loss of honour', i.e. loss of citizen rights, partial or total, either as a specific penalty or as the automatic (and reversible) consequence of owing a debt to the state.

Boule — ('Council') the board of 500 which acted as a steering group for the *Ekklesia*. The term is also used for the Areiopagos but only where the context precludes ambiguity.

choregia — public duty of chorus-producer at a festival; see also *leitourgia*.

demagogos a term for people active as speakers in the Assembly, anglicized as 'demagogue'.

demarchos 'demarch', the chief official of the deme; see also *demos*.

demos according to context the Athenian people as a whole or the masses. Inscriptions use the word to designate the popular Assembly (see also *Ekklesia*). *Demos* ('deme') is also used for the local units (urban districts or villages) which were the smallest political units of the democracy.

Demosion Sema public burial precinct for the war dead.

dikastai the 'jurors' empanelled in the people's courts (*dikasteria*); the translation is inexact, since they also performed the role of the modern judge in setting sentence.

dokimasia scrutiny to determine eligibility for: i. rights; ii. office or activity; iii. benefits.

eisangelia ('impeachment') a charge for political offences, laid before the Council or the Assembly according to the identity of the accused.

eisphora levy on the assets of the wealthy in time of war.

Ekklesia the formal meeting of the adult male citizens, usually rendered 'Assembly' in English; our sources use the word *demos* rather than *ekklesia* to refer to decisions by the Assembly.

ephebeia ('cadetship') a period of two years' military service performed by citizens immediately on reaching majority.

ephesis appeal, usually in Athens from a lower body or official to a court.

euthynai formal examination of the conduct of an official on termination of office.

genos (plural *gene*) 'clan', a notional kinship group larger than the *oikos* (see below), claiming descent from a common ancestor.

graphe 'indictment', literally '(charge in) writing', the most common kind of public action, often used in our sources as a generic term for public actions; the *graphe* covered offences which were felt to affect the polis generally and unlike the private action (*dike*), where only the

	individual affected could sue, prosecution was open to anyone (*ho boulomenos*).
graphe nomon me epitedeion theinai	'indictment for bringing an inexpedient law', a public action available in the fourth century against proposers of laws allegedly not in the public interest.
graphe paranomon	'indictment for illegality', a public action available against anyone moving a proposal in the Council or Assembly which contradicted existing legislation in substance or spirit; used against both laws and decrees in the fifth century but confined to decrees in the fourth century with the creation of *graphe nomon me epitedeion theinai* (see above).
graphe xenias	public action for 'being an alien' (*xenia*), i.e. for illegally usurping citizen rights.
ho boulomenos	generic term for the volunteer prosecutor in public actions, literally 'the one who wants/wishes', 'anyone who wants/wishes'.
Kerameikos	suburb to the north of the Agora, a favoured spot for elite tombs, also the location for the Demosion Sema (see above) and the funeral rites for the war dead.
leitourgia	('liturgy') public duty (usually expensive) allocated to the wealthy on the basis of assessed assets.
lexiarchikon grammateion	deme register of its members.
merismos	annual allocation of (their proportion of) state funds to officials in the fourth century.
metoikos	('metic') an alien resident in Attica; the residency tax he paid was called *metoikion*.
nomothetai	('legislators') panels used to scrutinize new legislation proposed and old legislation subject to repeal in the fourth century.
oikos	the family unit, the smallest kinship/social group.
ostrakismos	('potsherd vote') popular vote under which the individual receiving the largest share of the votes (cast by scratching a name on to a fragment of pottery) was exiled for ten years; obsolete by the end of the fifth century but never officially discontinued.

phratria — ('phratry') kinship group larger than the *genos* (see above) claiming descent from a common ancestor.

Pnyx — hill adjacent to the Acropolis and Areiopagos where the Assembly sat.

Polemarchos — ('Polemarch') one of the nine Archons, with duties especially in relation to resident aliens.

probouleuma — preliminary motion placed before the Assembly by the Council.

proedroi — ('chairmen') nine officials, members of Council, who presided over Assembly meetings in the fourth century.

prostates tou demou — 'champion of the *demos*', term for a prominent politician.

prytaneia — ('prytany') period of one tenth of the Athenian administrative year, designated from the term of office of the *prytaneis*.

prytaneis — standing committee of the Council, comprising the full contingent from one of the ten tribes, each tribe serving in rotation for one tenth of the year.

rhetor — 'public speaker', term used from the late fifth century for an active politician.

strategos — 'general', one of a board of ten military officials created by Kleisthenes; in the fifth century these were the most important public officials.

theorika — the money doled out from the *theorikon*.

theorikon — a state fund (the 'Theoric Fund') initiated to provide a dole for theatre attendance, subsequently extended to other types of festival and to public building projects.

Thesmothetai — the title of six of the nine Archons; see also *Archon*.

trierarchia — ('trierarchy') duty of responsibility for equipping and maintaining a trireme; see *leitourgia*.

Appendix 3

Some key events

621 Traditional date of Drakon's legislation
594 Traditional date of archonship of Solon
c. 560 Peisistratos comes to power
508/7 Reforms of Kleisthenes
490 First Persian invasion; battle of Marathon
480 Second Persian invasion; battle of Salamis
477 Foundation of Delian League
431 Outbreak of Peloponnesian War
421 Peace of Nikias between Athens and Sparta
415 Athenian expedition against Syracuse in Sicily
413 Sparta resumes war against Athens and fortifies Dekeleia in Attica; destruction of Athenian expeditionary force to Sicily
411 Regime of the Four Hundred at Athens
405 Destruction of the Athenian fleet at the battle of Aigospotamoi
404 Athens surrenders to Sparta; end of Peloponnesian War
404/3 Regime of the Thirty at Athens
403 Restoration of democracy
378 Foundation of Second Athenian League
357 Philip comes to power in Macedon; desultory hostilities commence between Athens and Macedon
357–355 Athens at war with members of the Second Athenian League (Social War)
346 Athenian embassies to Macedonia; conclusion of Peace of Philokrates with Philip
340 Athens declares war on Philip
338 Defeat of anti-Macedonian axis at Chaironeia; Philip creates League of Corinth with himself as its leader
336 Philip assassinated; Alexander succeeds to the throne of Macedon

334 Alexander invades Asia

323 Death of Alexander; Athens takes the lead in the Lamian War against Macedon

322 Anti-Macedonian axis decisively defeated at the battle of Krannon; Macedonian garrison installed and Athenian democracy dramatically curtailed

Index